TIM BURTON'S Corpse Bride

An Invitation to the Wedding

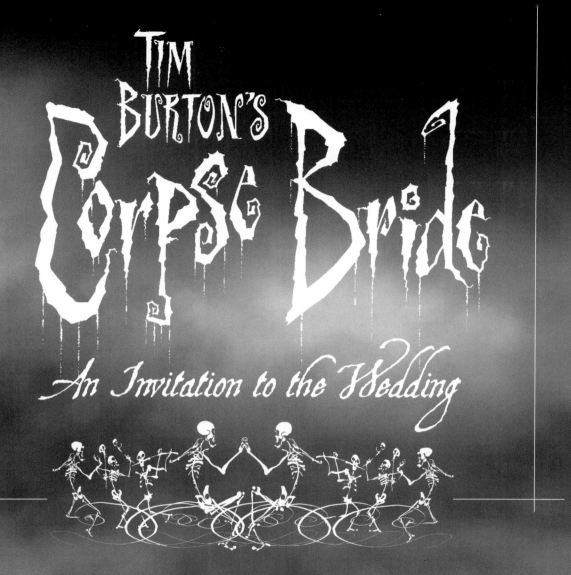

Tim Burton's Corpse Bride

An Invitation to the Wedding

TITAN BOOKS

Designed and Edited by TIMOTHY SHANER   *Text by* MARK SALISBURY

FIRST EDITION

10 9 8 7 6 5 4 3 2 1   10 9 8 7 6 5 4 3 2 1
1 84576 284 3 (Paperback)   1 84576 222 3 (Hardcover)

Published by
Titan Books
A division of
Titan Publishing Group Ltd
144 Southwark St
London
SE1 0UP

Visit our website: **www.titanbooks.com**

Did you enjoy this book? We love to hear from our readers. Please e-mail us at:
readerfeedback@titanemail.com or write to Reader Feedback at the above address.

To subscribe to our regular newsletter for up-to-the-minute news,
great offers and competitions, email: **titan-news@titanemail.com**

A CIP catalogue record for this title is available from the British Library.

Printed in the United States of America.

Also available from TITAN BOOKS

Alien vs. Predator: The Creature Effects of ADI
The Art of Batman Begins
The Art of X2: The Collectors Edition
The Art of X2: The Making of the Blockbuster Film
Caught in the Web: Dreaming Up the World of Spider-Man 2
Fantastic Four: The Making of the Movie
Giger's Alien
Giger's Film Design
Hellboy: The Art of the Movie
The Hellraiser Chronicles
Serenity: The Official Visual Companion

Contents

There's Going to Be a Wedding

by Tim Burton

rowing up, watching monster movies, I became a huge fan of Ray Harryhausen's work: *Jason and the Argonauts*, the Sinbad films, *20 Million Miles to Earth*. I knew his name before I knew any actor's name. Ray was, and remains, a very special artist and, watching his films, I could always feel the artistry behind his work. Like a lot of people, I was inspired by him and am where I am today in part because of him. Watching his films you were aware of the artistry, of the skill, and of the love he put into his work. He managed to imbue his monsters with more emotion than most of the actors in those movies. And if they didn't have a character, then he always gave his monsters a great death scene. They always had one final dying breath and one final shake of the tail, and you always felt bad for them. Growing up, watching these monsters in pain have their own tragic death was, in a way, a form of catharsis for my adolescent self.

OPPOSITE: The Corpse Bride accepts her ows. ABOVE: Burton's sketch of Paul the Head Waiter. RIGHT: Tim Burton on set.

7

When we were doing *Corpse Bride*, I was lucky enough to finally get to meet Ray. Johnny Depp, Helena Bonham Carter, and I visited his home and it was the most wonderful and delightful experience. I've been very lucky in my life to have been able to meet and work with people I've watched my whole life who have inspired me, people like Vincent Price, Christopher Lee, and Michael Gough, and in every case they have all turned out to be truly amazing and special people. Ray was no exception. And so it was a very special moment when he came to visit on the set of *Corpse Bride*. (I don't think much work got done that day.)

The idea for *Corpse Bride* came from an old folk-tale told to me by my friend Joe Ranft who I'd known since my student days at Cal Arts. Joe, who died shortly before we finished the movie, had worked at Disney, was storyboard supervisor on both *The Nightmare Before Christmas* and *James and the Giant Peach*, and had then worked his magic at Pixar. He was a master storyteller and when he told me this little story about a man caught between two women—one living, one dead—he knew it would interest me. This book is dedicated to him and all the amazing artists who worked on the film.

mr. bone jangles

OPPOSITE: Watercolor sketch by Tim Burton. ABOVE: Burton's sketches of Victor and Corpse Bride, Victoria, and Mr. Bonejangles

PART ONE

Land of the Living

A Very Happy Engagement

F rom *Pee-Wee's Big Adventure* to *Beetlejuice, Batman* to *Edward Scissorhands, Sleepy Hollow* to *Charlie and the Chocolate Factory*, Tim Burton has revealed himself to be one of cinema's true originals, constructing alternate worlds fueled by a childlike enchantment and the essential nature of dreams. A dazzling visionary whose work combines gothic horror, black comedy, and a whimsical, oddball imagination, his beautifully designed, highly stylized, idiosyncratic fairy tales can also be read as deeply personal visions, albeit ones that have enjoyed enormous critical and commercial success. And while there's both a touch of melancholy and a hint of darkness to his work, Burton's vision remains, fundamentally, a comic one, his audacious styling and macabre sense of humor producing delightfully ghoulish fantasies that are more Grimm's fairy tale than they are gruesome, films which have both a playfulness and an undeniable sweetness at their core.

Burton began his career at Walt Disney Studios in the early 1980s working as an animator on *The Fox and the Hound*, attempting to draw cute little foxes that, in his words, came out looking more like "roadkill," and later as a conceptual artist on films such as *The Black Cauldron*. And, in many ways, he's remained that animator at heart ever since.

By his own admission, he and the Disney regime at the time weren't the best fit, but thanks to the foresight of an enterprising executive who saw in him the potential, Burton was allowed to make *Vincent*, a five-minute black-and-white short about Vincent Malloy, a disturbed little boy obsessed with Vincent Price and Edgar Allan Poe, as Burton had been.

ABOVE: Producer Allison Abbate (left), directors Tim Burton and Mike Johnson at the Three Mills Studio in East London. OPPOSITE: Animator Phil Dale manipulates Victor.

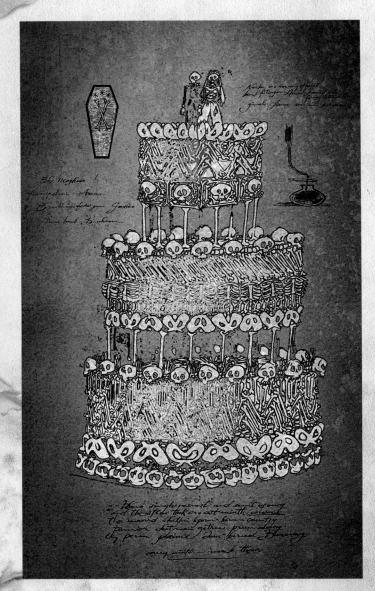

It was Burton's first foray into stop-motion animation outside of his home movies and wouldn't be his last.

Vincent found a home on the festival circuit and Burton swiftly moved on to directing live-action features although he managed to incorporate stop-motion animation into several of his subsequent films, among them *Pee-Wee's Big Adventure* and *Beetlejuice*, culminating in 1994's *The Nightmare Before Christmas*, which was, at the time, the most complex and elaborate stop-motion animated film ever created.

Until now that is, until *Corpse Bride*, Burton's latest venture into the world of stop-motion animation.

"I love stop-motion," he says. "The people who do this, they're artists, they're actors, they're breathing life into inanimate objects like Frankenstein and Pinocchio. And you can feel the artists' hands at work. It's kind of an unspoken, subconscious thing, which is why I like it; it's something you can't quite put words to. That's what's interesting about the medium. It's not to say you can't get it in cell animation or computer animation, you can, but there's a handmade quality that, for me, sets it apart from other things. There's a magic and mystery to stop-motion, a tactile quality, a handmade quality that gives it an emotional resonance for me. Maybe it's because I have nostalgia for it, but I do really believe there is that in the medium."

First seen in J. Stuart Blackton's *The Haunted House* in 1907, stop-motion animation hasn't changed all that much in close to a century. It's still the incredibly labor-intensive process that involves the frame-by-frame manipulation of a three-dimensional object—be it a puppet, model, even a human being—to make it to appear to move. The effect is based on an optical illusion. By moving an object a little bit at a time, shooting one frame of film, moving it a bit more, then shooting another frame and so on, the cumulative effect, once the film is projected at the standard rate of 24 frames per second, gives the illusion of movement. With one second of stop-motion requiring 24 minuscule changes of position, a full-length movie requires millions.

This painstaking art has produced many of cinema's classic moments, from King Kong climbing the Empire State Building, Fay Wray in his hairy hand, to Jason fighting the Argonauts for the Golden Fleece, to the plucky rebel alliance taking on the might of the Imperial Walkers on the snowy wastes of Hoth in *The Empire Strikes Back*. While the first celebrated exponent of stop-motion was Willis O'Brien who pioneered it as effects technique for *The Lost World* in 1925 and gave life to *King Kong* in 1933, it was his young protégé Ray Harryhausen whose name has become synonymous with the medium, having inspired and thrilled generations of moviegoers with films such as *20 Million Miles to Earth*, *Jason and the Argonauts*, *The Golden Voyage of Sinbad*, and *Clash of the Titans*. Burton, needless to say, is a huge Harryhausen fan.

As late as the mid-1990s, stop-motion animation was still being used as an effects technique in movies such as *The Terminator*, *Robocop*, and *Return of the Jedi*. But in today's computer-dominated era, stop-motion has largely fallen out of favor, rendered all but redundant by computer-generated imagery which has, in turn, had its own devastating effect on the traditional cell animation, the enormous popularity of CGI-animated movies like *Toy Story*, *A Bug's Life*, *Finding Nemo*, *The Incredibles*, *Robots*, and *Ice Age*, all but killing off two-dimensional animation.

And yet, stop-motion animation as an art form still survives, finding a home in television commercials, short films, and music videos, kept alive by the passion and patronage of people like Britain's Nic Park whose Oscar-winning *Creature Comforts* and Wallace and Gromit shorts led to the *Chicken Run* movie.

OPPOSITE: Prop artwork of the wedding cake created for the film. RIGHT: Mike Johnson (left) with veteran stop-motion animator Ray Harryhausen on the Victoria's Bedroom set.

Then, of course, there's Burton, whose lifelong love affair with stop-motion animation has paved the way for both Hollywood and audiences around the world to see the medium in a completely different light.

"Tim's ideas and his projects have brought stop-motion back into the public eye," declares Mike Johnson, Burton's co-director on *Corpse Bride*. "It was definitely fading out before *The Nightmare Before Christmas*. A lot of the effects, dinosaur effects and things like that, that it used to be used for, were all going to computer. *Nightmare* opened people's eyes to another use for it, just the charm of it that can't be achieved with computers."

It's this charm and old-fashioned artistry that's at the core of Burton's latest stop-motion animated feature *Corpse Bride*. Although the film uses the latest high-tech equipment, digital photography, and computer technology, it has remained faithful to stop-motion animation's low-tech roots.

"In light of the world we're living in now which is all about CGI and fast cutting and things looking super slick, we've really strived to make this movie look like it was made a hundred years ago," explains *Corpse Bride* producer Allison Abbate the artistic sensibility that's at the heart of the movie. "Even with our CGI stuff we're trying to put the quirks back in because we're using our technologies to make it seem more like stop-motion. The beauty of animation is that every frame is designed as opposed to visual effects where every shot is made to simulate real space and physics. We tried to put that beauty back into every frame, take it out of the realm of reality and put it into a more stylized space."

Story

While *The Nightmare Before Christmas* started life as a poem Burton had written and illustrated immediately after finishing work on *Vincent* in 1982, the concept for *Corpse Bride* came from an even older source.

The genesis was a 19th-century Eastern European folktale told to Burton by his

LEFT and OPPOSITE: Early sketches by Tim Burton of the Corpse Bride and Victor.

friend Joe Ranft, who had been storyboard supervisor on *The Nightmare Before Christmas* and the Burton-produced *James and the Giant Peach*, before moving to Pixar where he provided the story for *Toy Story* and *A Bug's Life*.

"Joe gave me the idea around the time of *Nightmare*," recalls Burton who had been looking for another project to do in stop-motion, "and it was minimal. There were no characters in it from what I recall, except for the Corpse Bride. It was like a little short story. And even though it was only a couple of paragraphs long, it captured my attention. It just seemed like it was right for that particular type of animation."

The tale concerned a young man traveling home in order to wed his fiancée. When his wedding ring winds up on the rotted finger of a murdered girl, who then returns from the grave and insists that she is the man's lawfully wedded wife, he's then forced to journey to the underworld to set things right, while his fiancée remains among the living, pining for his return.

For Burton, part of the success of *Nightmare* had been the emotional quality the film had managed to capture, particularly in terms of Sally. "I enjoyed the Sally character," he says. "It's nice to get emotion in animation. And I was trying to do something with that emotional quality to it again." Ranft's little tale seemed to offer the possibility "to make something else with this medium and to try and make it emotional and have an emotional resonance that you don't get in a lot of animated films. Also," he says, "I was thinking about expanding my female characters."

As his imagination began to percolate, Burton started putting pen and paint brush to paper, sketching out the first few characters for what would eventually become *Corpse Bride*, starting with the love-struck Corpse Bride herself, who was inspired by Elsa Lanchester's *Bride of Frankenstein* both visually and spiritually. Then came Victor Van Dort, the shy, nervy young groom-to-be who finds himself caught between two women, one alive, one dead; Victor's faithful fiancée,

Victoria Everglot; her money-grabbing parents, Finis and Maudeline Everglot; Bonejangles, a skeleton band leader in the mold of Sammy Davis Jr.; and Scraps, Victor's faithful (but deceased) mutt, who initially was conceived with flesh and bones but soon dropped the flesh part.

At around the same time, Burton asked Caroline Thompson who'd previously written the scripts for *Edward Scissorhands* and *The Nightmare Before Christmas* to flesh out the basic concept, with Thompson producing first a 25-page treatment then a screenplay that would later be reworked by Pamela Pettler and then John August, who wrote *Big Fish* and *Charlie and the Chocolate Factory* for Burton.

"One of the things Tim was so adamant about was finding a way to make a story that could be seen as scary or gruesome into a romantic fable about love and the truth of love not being skin deep," says producer Allison Abbate. "It's about freedom and expression and finding one's heart."

"The script took a long time, almost ten years to gestate," concurs Burton, "and went through a lot of different drafts." While the original folktale had been of Russian origin, Burton didn't want to set *Corpse Bride* in any particular country. "It was very clear to me that I wanted to keep that fairy-tale aspect," he says. "Even though it's got Victorian elements and largely a British cast, I didn't necessarily want to set it in a specific place."

As the script developed, so did the characters and their worlds. Victor would live in a grim, gray, austere milieu that owed its morals to Victorian England and its look to Eastern Europe. Dubbed the Land of the Living, it was a cold, unfriendly, impersonal, regimented kind of place. In contrast, Corpse Bride would, having "married" Victor, take him on a trip to the Land of the Dead, which, as conceived, was a brightly colored, joyful, vibrant world that was more alive than the Land of the Living. For Burton, the themes of inversion and of misperception were familiar ones, redolent of his other work. "That goes back to my childhood, feeling what people call normal is not normal and what people call abnormal isn't," he reveals. "Growing up in suburban America where people are afraid of death and then you have cultures like Mexico where they have Day of the Dead, it's such a fun holiday

ABOVE and OPPOSITE: Early sketches by Tim Burton of the Corpse Bride, Mr. Bonejangles, Paul the Head Waiter, Maggot, and the Black Widow.

where they celebrate it, it's fun, the skeletons are doing funny things, and I felt that's much more where I like to be. At the same time it's part of life and the cycling of life and not being so downbeat about it, even though it's sad, you want it to be kind of spiritual and hopeful and somewhat mysterious and beautiful. So it's that sort of thematic thing of the living world being much more dead than the dead world, and kind of playing those juxtapositions and those feelings that I remember having from very early on."

Just as important to Burton as finding the right setting for his story was getting the correct tone for the film's love triangle. "We needed to find the proper balance, because in several drafts Victor leaned too much toward Corpse Bride, others leaned more toward Victoria. With this kind of love triangle, you need to feel for both women. The audience needed to feel that Victor wasn't a jerk, he had a really tough decision to make. Finally I felt good that we got the right balance."

"I wanted to treat it more like a movie in a certain way," Burton continues, "a romantic fairy tale, a tragic romantic fairy tale, and I felt the seed from that from the Jack and Sally relationship in *Nightmare*, which I enjoyed and wanted to see if it could go off, different, and even more so in a way. There's a melancholy to it, but that's what I took from the original story. There's a sadness to it."

"What John August did was to take the prior versions of the script, which had varying amounts of quirkiness and comedy, and really put the passion and the heartbreak into it," explains producer Allison Abbate. "I found out later that the original fable really stresses Victoria's point of view and the Corpse Bride is more of a monstrous, villainous character. But there is a poignancy in the fable because the Corpse Bride's love for Victor triumphs in the end, and, although she gives him up, she knows that Victoria will love him enough for the both them.

"I didn't know that until Joe Ranft came to visit us and happened to mention it," she continues. "We just naturally gravitated to fleshing out Victoria's storyline because she gets the guy in the end. She is, in many ways, the heroine of the piece; she's feisty and she

OPPOSITE: Early sketch by Joe Ranft. RIGHT: Tim Burton sketch of the Everglots. FOLLOWING PAGES: Concept drawing by Chris Baker.

tries to save her man. We wanted to make Victoria a really strong character and not just the "other woman." If it was going to be satisfying for Victor to end up with her at the end of the movie, we needed to make Victoria appealing and worthy, and really believe that they were in love. It's rare in animation to depict this kind of emotion and tension. We weren't always going for the gag but going for the poignancy and subtlety of the relationships. The heart and acting in this movie rivals anything I think you'd see in a live-action movie."

Project Development

The *Nightmare Before Christmas* spent more than a decade in development before reaching the screen, which, as it turned out, was about the same time as *Corpse Bride*, the seeds of which were sown back in 1993 when Burton drew his initial sketches, although it would be two years until Warner Bros., for whom he was then directing *Mars Attacks!*, came on board. Even so, it wasn't until 2002 that the project finally came into focus, when Burton, then on location in Alabama directing *Big Fish*, began to amass the core creative team that would spearhead the project over the next three years.

Although *The Nightmare Before Christmas* was directed by Henry Selick, who Burton had known from their days at Disney together, the film, its sensibility, was clearly, undeniably Burton's, with his imprint on the look and design of its every frame and character. But having passed on helming *Nightmare*, partly because of his commitment to *Batman Returns*, Burton wanted to have more direct input into *Corpse Bride*. And yet for the day-to-day interaction with the animators, Burton required a codirector, hiring Mike Johnson who had worked on both *The Nightmare Before Christmas* and *James and the Giant Peach*, before going on to direct his own short *The Devil Went Down to Georgia* and an episode of the Eddie Murphy–voiced TV series *The P.J.s.* "He has a sensitivity," says Burton who was busy directing *Charlie and the Chocolate Factory* for much of *Corpse Bride*'s shoot. "He's done it,

ABOVE: Director Mike Johnson.

he's animated, he knows what the process is and there are not many people that get it and have done it and it's hard to communicate that to people when they don't come from that rarefied world."

"I think that Tim and Mike made a really good team," notes Abbate. "They were able to work really closely in preproduction so that once the shooting began they were very much in sync on what was needed for the animation."

Having Johnson on set allowed Burton the distance he needed. "Mike was there every day and this has been good for me, and I think it's worked out for the best. I was able to step back and look at it a bit more," he reflects, "to see it as fresh as possible and treat it more like I would treat a live-action movie where you look at dailies. And while you don't have the luxury on this of picking from a few takes of performance, you can start to see the shape of things and start to see what you need and don't need and try to form it, because like *Nightmare* it's very organic. The script has changed all the way through, little bits of humor and business, kind of goes back to the old days of Disney where it was story people shaping it as it goes. There's been a lot of that in this."

"One thing I learned working with Tim is the importance of making space for creative experimentation," says Johnson. "To stay loose and allow yourself time to play a bit. This isn't easy to do with the demands of a hectic schedule, but that creative spirit comes across on the screen, and I think it's a common thread in all of his films. It's obvious that he truly loves what he does. The process is as important as the final product."

Preproduction on *Corpse Bride* officially began in Los Angeles in February 2003 with Johnson joining production designer Alex McDowell (*Fight Club, Minority Report*) and art director Nelson Lowry, who'd worked with Johnson on *The P.J.s*, before moving to England where Burton is based, and Three Mills Studios in East London where they would be joined by *The Nightmare Before Christmas* director of photography Pete Kozachik and, in February 2004, producer Allison Abbate, a highly experienced animation veteran whose credits included *Iron Giant* and *Looney Tunes: Back in Action* and who, like Johnson and Kozachik, had worked on *The*

A home where they could live inside the Bride.

kidney?

maybe they use her dried up organs for furniture?

RIGHT: Early sketch of Accordian Man by Mike Johnson. ABOVE: Early sketch by Joe Ranft.

Nightmare Before Christmas as artistic coordinator. "I have wanted to get back into stop-motion ever since the *Nightmare* days, and when this opportunity arose to work so closely with Tim again, I jumped at the chance. His story sensibility and visual style are incredible. He can look at a story sequence and immediately know how to make it better."

Storyboards

On live-action movies, the storyboard process varies from film to film, director to direc-tor. Some filmmakers prefer to storyboard every shot, others use them for complicated special effects sequences only. In animation, however, storyboards are crucial because "there can be less emphasis on the script as a final source of story material," says *Corpse Bride* storyboard supervisor Jeff Lynch. "And sometimes you'll even be starting from a concept. In our case we had a really marvelous script from John August."

Even so, the *Corpse Bride* script was, says Burton, "an organic thing," with ideas, characters, jokes, and sight gags being added throughout the filmmaking process, contributed by everyone from Burton, Ranft, and Johnson to the storyboard artists themselves who worked with Lynch to break down the script, scene by scene, into thousands of drawings.

The process served a variety of purposes, not least providing the filmmakers with a previsualization of the entire movie, but also to see if the script and the characters were working. The storyboard artists were allowed sizeable input into the direction of the story. "It's a matter of sort of sitting down with the team and talking about the characters and plot

points," Lynch notes. "What are the things that have to happen to take you from A to B to C to resolution? Then you have discussions about the characters. Who is this character? What do they want? Where are they going? What are they like when they finish? What have they learned? What does this character learn from this character? You try to bring them alive so that you can understand them. And the more you know about your characters, the more you can see whether it's true or not."

"I think it was critical that we had such a strong team of English and European storyboard artists," notes producer Allison Abbate. "They brought a great sense of language and acting that we wouldn't have had from a big American crew. They understood the more subtle Victorian humor and often came up with the strongest moments in the film."

After the initial pass on the storyboards is completed, the boards are then photographed and turned into what's known as a story reel—a moving storyboard. This is then synched up to whatever music and/or voices that have been recorded thus far to produce an initial version of the movie which can be added to and amended as necessary. "That's when you learn the most," says Lynch, "because then you can sense the rhythms of the film and the rhythms of the characters, which you don't always see when you're looking at it sequence by sequence or even looking at an entire act."

"Stop-motion is so time consuming that we can't afford coverage and multiple takes," says Johnson. "We get one take per

OPPOSITE and ABOVE: "Victor in the Woods" storyboard sequence by Tim Watts. RIGHT: Final film still of the sequence.

shot, and it had better be good. That's why most of our editorial decisions are made during the story reel process where we have the freedom to experiment with different ideas.

Sometimes it takes a while to dial it in. It's not uncommon for a sequence to be storyboarded 50 different ways. Luckily, our storyboard team had an endless reserve of pencils, patience, and bulldog tenacity."

The storyboard artists also worked closely with the editorial team to build the timing and acting of each scene. "The story reel is really the road map for the animators to follow," says Abbate. "We were lucky to find a really strong group of artists to lay that foundation."

It was during this stage, Lynch says, that it was considered necessary to make Victoria a stronger, more resourceful character in order to compete with the Corpse Bride for Victor's affections. "The Corpse Bride was so interesting, so dynamic and so colorful, we thought, How can this other woman compete?" he recalls. "You have this hot woman, who's full of life, even though she's dead, but she's got all this vitality and everything. Then you have Victoria who's the product of the Victorian era. So we started looking at the scales going, Why is he going back to Victoria? What can we do to strengthen her character, to make her more strong-willed or to make her more dedicated to him? So that as an audience member you're not going, 'Hey, forget the other girl, go with the Corpse Bride. She's the one that's fun.' That's what we were starting to fear. You want to feel that pull back and forth between the characters so you can understand how Victor could vacillate between the two women."

ABOVE: Mike Johnson and storyboard artist Chris Butler (left), discuss a sequence. OPPOSITE: Storyboard panel by Sharon Smith with inset of film still.

By the same token, however, Corpse Bride needed to be seen as somewhat sympathetic, especially since she kidnaps Victor and takes him under duress to the Land of the Dead. "You want to see how he could be kidnapped but then grow to appreciate and to become close to the Corpse Bride while still remaining in love with Victoria," says Lynch. "And then what happens if that love is no longer something that he can pursue? You don't

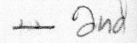

top that infernal coughing !!"

29

want to be feeling like he's going to jump with whatever woman is available, because then you're thinking, What a putz. But if he stands too strongly in one area, then there's nowhere to go with the other character. So it's this fine line of how does Victor seem true to his character and true to his first love, but still chooses to stay with this other person?"

Creating Characters

In order to flesh out his initial designs into fully realized three-dimensional characters, Burton approached acclaimed puppet makers Ian Mackinnon and Pete Saunders, who operate out of Manchester, England, and whose credits include *Bob the Builder*, *The Wind in the Willows*, and numerous commercials. "They do such beautiful work. Very sensitive and textural," says Burton who'd worked with them originally on *Mars Attacks!* when his plan was to do the Martians using stop-motion animation. In the end, given the complexity of the film, stop-motion proved unfeasible and the Martians ended up being all computer-generated, but Burton had enjoyed their collaboration. "Like everybody, they do commercials, they do *Bob the Builder* and things like that, but they rarely get the chance to show what they can *really* do," he says. "They've got a good group of sculptors and they really do amazing work. I saw that based on the puppets they had done for *Mars Attacks!*. There was no question in my mind that these were the guys to do it."

LEFT: Tim Burton's original sketch for the Corpse Bride.
BELOW: Preliminary sketch of Land of the Living characters by Carlos Grangel.
OPPOSITE: Grangel's color studies for zombies in the Land of the Dead.

KIND OF DEAD PEACOCK

DEAD PIGEON

KUAK KUAK

31

NEEDS
BETTER
DESIGN
FOR RIB
CAGE

"We were working in Los Angeles on *Mars Attacks!* back in 1995 when Tim first showed us some sketches from *Corpse Bride*," recalls Mackinnon. "It was obviously a project that was dear to his heart and he was hoping to get the movie made. We heard nothing about it for quite a number of years and then [in December 2001] he called up, said he was in London and could we come and discuss the project again."

Burton showed them the character drawings he'd done as well as a Corpse Bride maquette that Rick Heinreichs, a long-time friend and collaborator who'd helped create the puppets for *Vincent*, had been a visual consultant on *The Nightmare Before Christmas*, and had later served as production designer on *Sleepy Hollow* and *Planet of the Apes*, had built many years before. They, says Mackinnon, gave them an indication that he was looking for something a little bit different from the puppets in *The Nightmare Before Christmas*. "Tim had these sketches of the lead characters and the great thing was the characters were already there: Victor, Victoria, and the Corpse Bride," Mackinnon remembers. "They were sort of quick pencil sketches and paintings but he'd captured the look of the characters. But how they would translate into puppets was a bit of an unknown," confirms Saunders. "His style of working is to get ideas down quickly, and the sketches are imbued with such great characters but we needed to have those refined."

ABOVE: Master puppet manufacturers Ian Mackinnon (left) and Pete Saunders. RIGHT: Key artists in character creation (from left to right) Carlos Grangel, Huy Vu, Carlos' brother Jordi and Carlos Burges, type designer. OPPOSITE: Grangel's concepts for the skeleton band on his preferred medium of cardboard boxes.

The solution turned out to be right under their noses. During a visit to Mackinnon and Saunders' studio in late 2002, Burton caught sight of some sketches that Carlos Grangel, a leading animation character designer, had done for *Periwig Maker*, an Oscar-nominated short film for which they'd built the puppets. Originally a comic-strip artist, the Spanish-born Grangel had moved into animation with Steven Spielberg's Amblin Studios in the 1990s, becoming a much sought-after character designer in the animation field, working on a number of DreamWorks

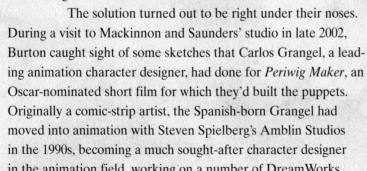

animated projects, including *The Prince of Egypt, Shark Tale*, and *Madagascar*. On the strength of his *Periwig Maker* drawings and a meeting with Burton, Grangel was brought on to help refine and develop Burton's sketches into a complete cast of characters who would populate the film's Land of the Living and Land of the Dead.

"Carlos is a great designer," Burton says. "My sketches are often quite crude but he was really sensitive about taking things and trying to understand what the feeling and the look of it was and expand upon it. The biggest challenge was the human characters. On *Nightmare*, none of the characters were really human and I always find with stop-motion when you try and do human characters they're really unappealing. But Carlos really helped flesh things out."

"He handed me a bunch of sketches, maybe six, seven, eight characters, and they were lovely, very loose, great lines, some of them with a bit of water color," Grangel recalls. "What is great about Tim is he can do the entire film himself but he wanted to share his vision and his way of doing things. I started working on the film right away."

That was in January 2003 and over the course of the next few months Grangel and the team at his small Barcelona-based studio (which included his brother Jordi and Carlos Burges, who came up with the film's typography and logo), working in close conjunction with the team at Mackinnon and Saunders, began conceptualizing the cast of *Corpse Bride*. "I remember Tim saying he wanted to see this film as a very artistic film, that he wanted to see the thumbprint on the face of the characters," Grangel notes. "And I remember him saying that every character has to be interesting. Main character, secondary characters, and incidental characters, the more interesting the better, the richer the film will be. So when you see the movie you find every character is interesting—at least to look at."

Burton was keen to differentiate the look of the characters in *Corpse Bride* from those in *The Nightmare Before Christmas*, although they still had to adhere to his signature style: large eyes, small pupils, long, spindly legs, and tiny feet. "For me, one of the biggest challenges working on this with Victor and the Corpse Bride was that I didn't want them to seem like a reworking of the Jack Skellington and Sally characters from *Nightmare*, even though you can see the seed of them within those," codirector Mike

LEFT: Tim Burton's original sketch for Corpse Bride.
OPPOSITE: Grangel's early sketches for Corpse Bride.

Johnson says. "We had to keep them within Tim's world but try to take them as far from the *Nightmare* look as we could and still make them feel Burton-esque." Grangel started on the Land of the Living characters using a series of Victorian photographs—high-society portraits and wedding albums—that McDowell and Johnson had chosen as inspiration. "They were all already caricatures with the long hats and the feathers and all that, and I wanted to add more on that style," he says. Although, as Burton previously discovered, "Human characters, no matter what you do, are always difficult to do. With an animal you can always push it and make it funny and graphic, and those characters were tough, particularly Victoria and Corpse Bride, they were the hardest."

The look of Corpse Bride herself had been set very early on in Burton's initial sketches, but there was still work to do before everyone was completely happy. According to Grangel, Corpse Bride was the character that both he and Burton did the most designs for because she had to be ghoulish but not gruesome, dead but beautiful—a challenge for any designer. "That was very hard to make something nice and yet it's a zombie. We did her in a way more pretty than she was in both Tim's early sketches and our early sketches. We didn't want it to go the gross way, the gruesome way, at the same time we didn't want to make something corny. It had to be a zombie but it had to be pretty and it had to be elegant and she had to be very sophisticated."

"Corpse Bride had an interesting evolution," Johnson agrees. "You can see the core of her in Tim's first sketch but she went back and forth through a few different extremes. At one point she was much more zombielike, crustier, covered with roots; then there was a design phase where she

ABOVE: Grangel's color concepts for Corpse Bride. RIGHT: The final maquette built by Mackinnon and Saunders. OPPOSITE: Grangel's concepts for the Cooks. FOLLOWING PAGES: Grangel's ideas for inhabitants of the Land of the Dead.

MEDUSA
HEAD

LUNCH TIME

BARBECUE
KIT

SALAD
DRESSING

was much more corpselike; and then she swung back to this more 30s, 40s Hollywood glamor look which is what we were going for. Also, we were all obsessed about each detail, even the veil and her dress took a long, long time to get it to where it needed to be."

It was the same with Corpse Bride's hair color, which was yellow until very late in the day when Burton opted for blue "to tie her together a bit more, so she had much more of a singular color scheme," he says. "We experimented with a few things but ultimately that felt right."

Unlike a lot of cell-animation movies whose characters tend to resemble those actors who are voicing them, stop-motion doesn't follow suit. And yet there's something more than a little familiar about a number of *Corpse Bride* cast members. Grangel admits to putting some of Christopher Lee from the Dracula movies ("very sinister, kind of vulture-like") into his designs for Pastor Galswell whom Lee voices, and says he had Helena Bonham Carter, who would go on to provide the voice for the Corpse Bride, in mind when designing the character. "Tim suggested Helena for the voice but I did some sketches that were more Helena than some of Tim's early ones in which the head was kind of more pointy and the chin more a triangular shape. I wanted to add that oval fore-head that Helena has on her face, it's really pretty."

"It's funny," Johnson notes, "a lot of people say, "of course Victor looks like Johnny Depp or Corpse Bride looks like Helena Bonham Carter," but at the point when these characters were designed we still had not cast the film, although I think at the back of everyone's mind we kind of hoped that's where it would go."

As with Corpse Bride, Victor didn't change much from Burton's original sketch, and while he looks not unlike Johnny Depp who voices him, anyone who's seen Burton's

stop-motion short *Vincent* will notice a striking similarity between the two characters, with Victor an adult version of Vincent, who, it must be said, also looks not unlike Burton himself. "I can see that," he says. "My drawing style is pretty specific and fairly limited, and Victor did sort of end up being a grown-up looking version of Vincent because basically that's the way I draw. Spiritually, it sort of makes sense in the type of project it is as well."

Victoria, who would eventually be voiced by the British actress Emily Watson, proved to be another interesting design chal-lenge according to Johnson because the character physically had to hold her own against Corpse Bride. "Throughout the design stage I was concerned she would be a little too bland to share the spotlight with the other two," he reflects. "But her design was so simple and elegant that once we saw her move in the ani-mation test, she just came to life. It is the contrast of her simplic-ity versus all the detail in Corpse Bride that works for her."

Another two of Burton's earliest creations who didn't go through much of a design evolution were Finis and Maudeline Everglot, the short and stout and skinny and very tall parents of Victoria, who would be voiced by Albert Finney and Joanna Lumley. "Finis is one of my favorite characters," says Johnson. "He was sort of the purest coming out of the gate from Tim's first sketch, the character was there and just through the sculpting process and finally the puppet and the voice he just seemed to me the one that was there from the beginning and took the least amount of experimentation to nail. Maudeline too. They're very similar to his original designs and I think he was going for an extreme contrast in shape." As a result, Victor's par-ents, William and Nell Van Dort (voiced by Paul Whitehouse and Tracey Ullman), proved a tough design to crack. "It took a lot of searching to find characters that could stand along-side Victoria's parents, who had such a strong design sense," says Johnson, "a lot of work from Carlos and his team."

One of the unique aspects of Grangel's creative process is the fact he drew all his

OPPOSITE and RIGHT: Grangel's concepts for Elder Gutknecht, Mr. Bonejangles, and Maggot on his preferred medium of the back of card-board cereal boxes.

Corpse Bride character designs on the back of breakfast cereal boxes. But not just any cereal boxes, specifically Von's Krispy Rice and Kellogg's Special K. "These are two favorites," he says. "Almost 85 percent of the characters suggested for *Corpse Bride* were done on those ones. Some boxes are darker than others and I have to get the right one." For Grangel, the patina, the gray of the cardboard helped him present the characters in the best possible light, using pastels and colored pencils to give his drawings a look that worked well for the film's mix of Victorian and Grimm's fairy tale.

Having produced a cast of characters for the Land of the Living that everyone agreed on, Grangel moved on to those inhabiting the underworld, whom, he says, were easier to conjure. "In the Land of the Dead, you have the skeletons and the zombies and you can go more wild, you can go more graphic, and you can go more crazy."

Of the many underworld characters, several stand out from the ghoulish crowd. There's Elder Gutknecht, the skeletal leader of the underworld voiced by Michael Gough who played Alfred in Burton's Batman films, and Bonejangles, the skeleton band leader who, as with Oogie Boogie from *Nightmare*, was inspired by a musician, in this case, Rat Pack member and comedian, Sammy Davis Jr. Along with his skeleton band, Mr. Bonejangles reveals the tragic story of Corpse Bride in a Cab Calloway-inspired jazz number called "The Remains of the Day" written and performed by Burton's regular musical collaborator Danny Elfman.

Then there's Maggot, who spends his time inside Corpse Bride's head, doling out advice and sarcasm in equal measures, whose personality and voice were inspired by the late, great character actor Peter Lorre. "From the very beginning Tim wanted the Maggot to be a Peter Lorre-esque character, and we had a good time working with that and it went through various design changes," says Johnson. "Sometimes it looked a little too much like a caterpillar; sometimes it looked a little too much like a snake; so we just had to find the middle ground where that was working."

Whenever Maggot goes, so does Black Widow Spider, an affable arachnid with a heart of gold, voiced by Jane Horrocks. "We weren't really sure what her character was, up until the third draft," Johnson admits. "We knew from the drawings that we wanted them to be a team but we didn't know if she was going to be a motherly type or this seasoned voice

of wisdom to the Corpse Bride. So it wasn't until Jane Horrocks got involved and gave us some options with the voice that that character came together.

"Paul the Head Waiter, voiced by Paul Whitehouse, was another of Burton's earliest creations that again didn't change much from his first sketch," Johnson continues. "He went through a few mutations along the way but sort of came back around to where he started. Not quite sure what the inspiration was, other than the fact Tim wanted a French waiter carried by beetles."

In all, Gragnel and his studio ended up designing 82 different *Corpse Bride* characters although not all of them were ultimately used as the script went through many changes and characters were dropped. "The great thing I think Carlos brought to a lot of the other characters, the background characters, because there's a lot that don't have a lot of screen time, was you can look at them and you can *see* the character," says Burton. "You see some of the relatives who've come for the wedding, and you just get it right away, and I felt very good about that."

Once an initial lineup of around 26 or so characters, mainly from the Land of the Living, had been approved by Burton, it was time for the team at Mackinnon and Saunders, with Grangel continuing to supervise their designs, to begin the process of translating them into three-dimensional puppets. This was easier said than done because of the extreme proportions inherent in Burton's original creations.

"Tim's characters are always a challenge to build as a three-dimensional model because they tend to be rather tall and skinny and tend to have very, very tiny feet which is

ABOVE: Mackinnon and Saunders lead sculptor Noel Baker. RIGHT: Some of the detailed notes kept for each character for the puppet sculptors to follow.

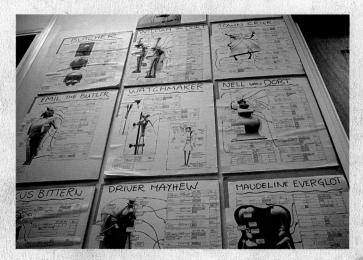

quite unique. Model animation characters tend to be shorter and have huge feet just because gravity helps hold them down," reveals Mackinnon, whose team would sketch turnarounds of each character before then sculpting a series of maquettes that Carlos would get photographs of and draw on and make notes, along with Johnson and Burton. These would be passed back to Mackinnon and Saunders for further refinement; the process continuing until each sculpt was approved. Only then would the puppet-making stage begin, with molds made and armatures built. "We had to look at different ways of engineering the joint system that we use inside the models and how they would support the weight of the character." Part of the problem was that the characters' heads were all about 25 to 30 centimeters away from the floor. "The animator is reaching up all the time trying to manipulate a head and there's an awful lot of leverage, so the puppet has to be secured well to the set."

ABOVE: Tim Burton inspects the first maquettes in 2003. RIGHT ABOVE: Composite image of the "maquette" cast at Mackinnon and Saunders. OPPOSITE BELOW LEFT: Angela Kiely applies paint to Victoria's dress. OPPOSITE BELOW RIGHT: Grangel works on a maquette.

"We were pushing the boundaries on what physics allowed," agrees Johnson. "The hinges and joints needed to hold these puppets in place were much thinner than normal. It's characteristic of Tim's style that these characters have very narrow, tapering legs and tiny feet and that doesn't lend itself well to stop-motion where the puppets have to support themselves. Once Carlos got involved in the design those extremes were pushed even further, so we had very thin, thin joints on certain characters. Scraps was a good example of where the puppet makers really had to stretch themselves to create mechanical joints on such a tiny scale."

Ironically, it's here computer technology would prove useful. For those puppets that couldn't support their own weights due to their thin legs or tiny feet, the animators would use metal rigs to keep them upright, rigs that would then be removed digitally.

In terms of their armatures, the jointed, movable metal skeletons, typically steel or aluminium, that allow them to be positioned as required, the *Corpse Bride* puppets weren't that dissimilar from those created for *The Nightmare Before Christmas*. What was

different was what went on the *outside* of them. While most stop-motion puppets are covered with either foam latex or a silicon-based skin, for *Corpse Bride*, Mackinnon and Saunders produced skins that were a combination of the two. "They had a substructure of foam latex which gives a lot of malleability," says Saunders, "and on top of that they had bonded to them a very thin coating of silicon, which gave a very smooth and clean finish and which was more suitable for the

ABOVE: Corpse Bride hair tests. BELOW LEFT: Mold with Corpse Bride "Tiara." BELOW RIGHT: Cordelia O'Neill applies "hair" to the underlying armature to create movement.

paint finishes that Tim and Carlos were driving for, for the look of the characters. And some of these combination skins had tiny, tiny joints actually cast into them. It was almost like a bionic skin in a way."

The results were plain to see. "If you look at *Nightmare*, the wrinkly latex skin makes them look like puppets," says producer Allison Abbate. "These are a silicon latex combination that really makes it look like the Corpse Bride has got dewy beautiful skin, and to me that's what makes it really seem like she's alive." Even Corpse Bride's hair was something special. "Her hair is very complicated," continues Abbate. "That hair is made from many different tendrils of mohair and silicon, it's like a puppet itself."

"It was crafted onto a three-part wig base," explains Saunders, "and had a whole system of malleable wires affixed to this metallic skullcap that was actually bolted on to the head—her tiara had access points where you could bolt it to the wig. It was like a metallic skullcap that had an organic feel to it when it was all assembled."

The method employed in *Nightmare* to give its puppets a full range of facial movement was a series of replacement heads, each with a different expression, that would allow them to emote, speak, or sing by, literally, the animators replacing their heads when necessary. Although the result was extremely successful, the technique brought with it its own set of problems. "With replacement animation the animation is predetermined by the voice track," explains Mackinnon, "and by the sculpts that have to be done. There's only a limited number of sculpts that you can do for each character, so the animator then has to work with that set number and they can't alter those facial expressions."

Johnson was determined

to try a different method for *Corpse Bride*. "At first Mackinnon and Saunders wanted to go with replacement heads," he says, "but my concern was the human characters, to have a flesh-colored face that has subtle shading painted on it, to do that as replacement animation I didn't think it would hold up under tight close-ups, projected on the big screen." What he had in mind was something akin to the mechanical heads Mackinnon and Saunders had pioneered for a series of commercials to give their puppets a far greater range of expression. The trouble was, Mackinnon and Saunders had only produced them on a larger scale than what was needed for *Corpse Bride*—tennis ball–size compared to the Ping Pong ball–size required by Johnson. "It had never really been pushed to this level before," he explains, "having the mechanics be small enough to fit with the scale of these puppets. It gives us a much more expressive look than replacement animation, which is a little more locked off and predetermined. It's a little more time-consuming than replacement animation, but the look is more subtle and more expressive."

Initially Saunders wasn't even sure it could be done. "But Mike was very insistent and had more faith in our abilities than perhaps we did. He was right, and I'm glad he stuck to his guns because the style of puppet is very different from *Nightmare*." What Saunders pioneered for *Corpse Bride* was a geared mechanism inside the puppet heads, similar to the workings of a Swiss watch. "We ended making these very complicated heads with little gears that open and close the jaws and a system of small pulleys that enable the characters to smile or frown. They have little lip paddles so that you can articulate the lips into different shapes to get convincing lip-synch. There's a good deal of sophistication packed into these tiny puppets." By inserting an Allen wrench into a socket in the ears of the puppets, the animators could control various facial movements. If you put the key into the left ear and turned it in one direction, it would make the puppet smile on the left-hand side of the face; if you turned it the other way it would make the corner of the mouth on that side of the face droop down, giving the puppet a slightly sad expression, and vice versa on the other side.

ABOVE: The final Corpse Bride figure with hair.

The result offered Johnson an amazing range of subtle emotions at his animator's disposal, which in turn lead to much more convincing performances. Which was just as well, because Burton's preference was for big, open eyes and lots of close-ups. "Often, if you're working on a TV series it wouldn't matter how many stages there are to a blink, but on the big screen they've got to give a real subtle performance," Mackinnon states. "It required teams of people to carefully cut out little eyelids and then hand stick on eyelashes onto each one. We have the most beautiful sculpts of Victor and Victoria and if you had put a heavy eyelid on it, it would have spoiled the whole face. So every element, every detail had to be done precisely, even though the viewer isn't going to be aware of the intricacies of the process. They're just going to see a character blinking and not even think about the amount of hours and weeks that were spent on that one blink."

In all, Mackinnon and Saunders produced 40 of these intricate mechanical heads for Corpse Bride, Victor, and Victoria. The remaining characters and remaining 160 or so puppets utilized one of three different types of head. Some were very simple skeletal heads where the jaw simply opened and closed; others were ball-and-socket heads with tiny little joints that articulated the lips and the eyebrows, and which, Saunders says, were every bit as painstaking, tricky, and complex to do as the mechanical heads. Then there were the puppets such as the Town Crier and Nell Van Dort, Victor's mother, who, as per *Nightmare*, relied on

OPPOSITE: The Land of the Living cast heads. ABOVE: Mechanical innerworks of the latex head. BELOW: Some of the many facial expressions achieved with the new Allen wrench technology.

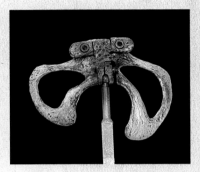

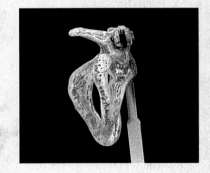

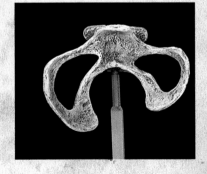

replacement mouths to perform a number of very extreme facial expressions. "We knew [Nell] was going to be a very loud, brassy character and with these mechanical faces one of the things we're giving up is extremes in the mouth shapes," Johnson reflects. "We knew that Nell would have to open her mouth to sing and yell, and we decided that replacement mouths for her would be more effective."

Equally challenging as the mechanical heads were the skeleton puppets Mackinnon and Saunders created for Bonejangles and his band. "They were difficult because there was no way you could hide the substructure underneath it," explains Mackinnon who looked at stop-motion skeletons designed by Ray Harryhausen to see what he could learn. "You can see right through the skeletons, the ribcages are open, and Tim and Carlos would want the bones to be shaved down so that they were so fine and delicate. There's very little holding them together at times. Usually the armatures inside the puppets are covered with skin or fabric and when you suddenly have to produce a naked skeleton it's difficult because there's no compromise to hide the metal structure inside it.

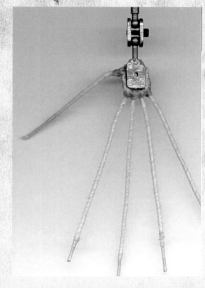

"And the more Carlos pushed the designs, the thinner they became. There was very little compromise from the original drawings that Tim did and Carlos interpreted to the finished puppets. If something was drawn with a tiny little ankle or a tiny little neck then that's the way it had to be developed as a puppet, and there were very few occasions where we said, This is going to have to change. So we were trying to defy gravity with bits of metal trying to make something that would eventually be a practical puppet that the animators could use. Plus they had to do a lot; they were going to be dancing, swapping parts, and reconfiguring into different characters."

Less dynamic but no less difficult was Elder Gutknecht, skeletal leader of the underworld, the puppets for which were made almost entirely out of brass. "There was very little room to cast any material over the top of it, which is quite unusual for the way we approach armatures," Mackinnon reveals. "So what you see is the ball-and-socket armature hand painted to disguise the joints as much as possible."

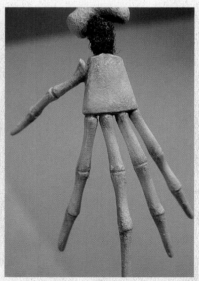

OPPOSITE: Details of Elder Gutknecht's hip and skull, and two views of the finished maquette. RIGHT: Detail of Mr. Bonejangles' armature, above, and the latex-covered armature below.

PART TWO

Land of the Dead

THE BEYOND

Land of the Dead

1. Elder's House
2. Public House
3. Butcher
4. Columns
5. Barber Shop
6. Gate House
7. Baker & Tailor
8. Colonnade

MOOR OF THE MORTIFIED

THE LAND BEYOND BELOW

Designing Worlds

The story of *Corpse Bride* takes place in two very distinct worlds: the Land of the Living where Victor, Victoria, and their respective parents reside, and the Land of the Dead, the underworld to which Corpse Bride takes Victor after their sudden marriage.

To create these two radically different environments, production designer Alex McDowell and art director Nelson Lowry spent an initial three months working in Los Angeles with a team of designers and concept artists, including Huy Vu, Luc Desmarchelier, and Simón Varela, using Burton's original sketches and Carlos Grangel's drawings as their templates. "Tim's original ideas gave us a sense of what the world should be like," Lowry explains. "Once you have a strong character design, the world follows closely behind it. The characters have to look embedded in the background."

Both thematically and visually, *Corpse Bride* is about inversion, with the Land of the Living a gray, dead place where the people are lifeless, hopeless, and sad, while the Land of the Dead is full of vivacious dead people with a lust for life and joy. As to how to present that designwise, McDowell and his team spent a long time experimenting with different ideas. "It was a refinement process starting with a very big open sky and just trying lots of crazy stuff and distilling them and getting something that would really work with the characters,"

PREVIOUS PAGE: Simón Varela's illustration of the Land of the Dead. ABOVE and RIGHT: Huy Vu's underworld character concepts. OPPOSITE: Land of the Dead map done early in production by Chris Baker. FOLLOWING PAGES: Some of the many concept drawings by Huy Vu.

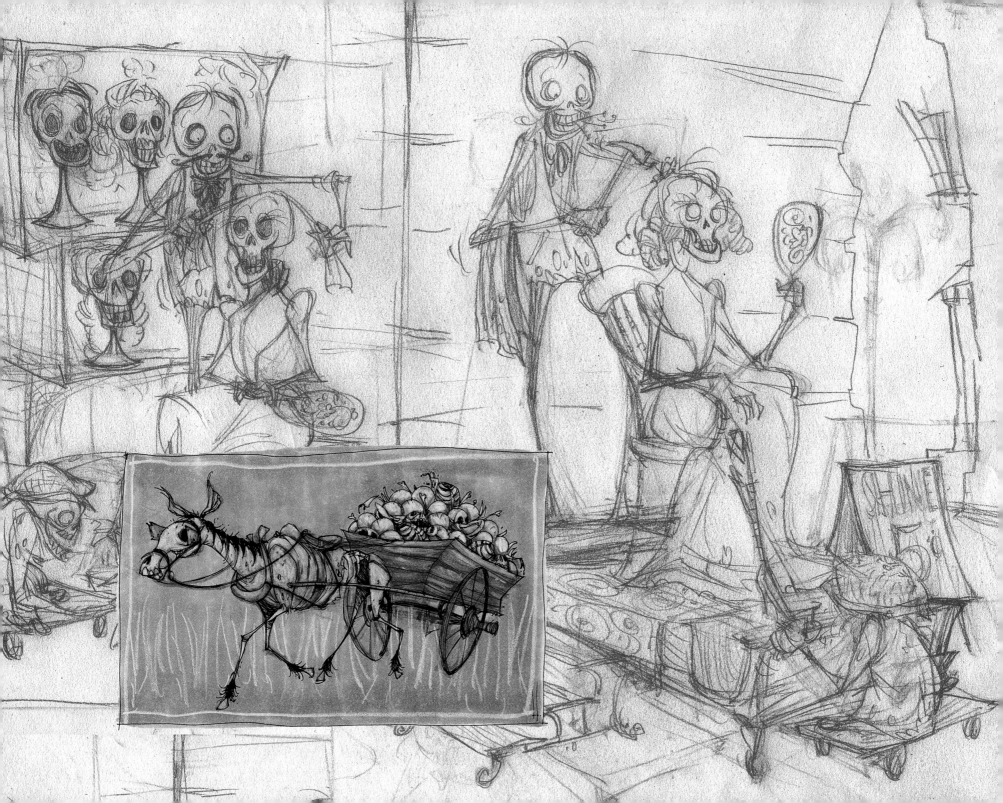

Lowry recalls. "At that point Carlos was really turning out the characters, so suddenly we had a whole cast. As soon as we did anything that was too realistic and put the characters in there, they looked really kind of monstrous and odd. And if we did something too crazy and put them in, they looked too realistic. We had to find a balance."

Corpse Bride was McDowell's first time working in the field of stop-motion, and after the initial three months in Los Angeles, moved on to Steven Spielberg's *The Terminal*, although he rejoined Burton on *Charlie and the Chocolate Factory*, handing over the design reins to Lowry, who later moved to England with the production. Unlike live-action design, stop-motion requires a little less in the way of detail. As Lowry explains, "In order for the audience to know what they're looking at, you have to pull back a little bit. On a live-action feature you can have big extravagant models with lots of detail but it doesn't really work so well in stop-motion, so it's finding images that are very clean and illustrative."

One of McDowell's early design concepts that didn't make it into the final film but proved the creative spark for all that was to follow was an image of a thin crust around a spherical world with the Land of the Living above the crust and the Land of the Dead directly below. "So the Land of the Living and the Land of the Dead were actually foot to foot and people were essentially upside down in the Land of the Dead," he states. "Although we didn't hold on to that idea, it set a lot of ideas in motion about using roots as trees, for example, so the tree above the ground became the

ABOVE and LEFT: Concept sketches by Huy Vu.
OPPOSITE: Early Simón Varela illustration of the Pub in the Land of the Dead.

tree below the ground and there was this kind of mirroring between the two lands. The Land of the Dead is almost a pastiche of the Land of the Living. You have a statue in the Land of the Living, but in the Land of the Dead it's a skeleton on a skeleton of a horse. And you have buildings that are sort of the decayed version of the colorful version, almost like the color has bled down through the ground and come to rest on the buildings in the Land of the Dead."

Ultimately the Land of the Living took its design cues from Victorian England mixed with an Eastern European sensibility, inspired by the original folktale. As reference, McDowell amassed a library of books on 18th- and 19th-century Russian painting, as well as Eastern European and Victorian architecture. Another prime reference source was

ABOVE: Simón Varela's concept illustration for the Land of the Living forest.

Victorian-era photography, the austerity of their subjects, coupled with the various methods of the time—hand-tinted daguerreotypes and glass photography with its soft focus quality—proving a real boon to the design team.

"My approach generally to design is to take relatively disparate elements and hope, by sort of thrusting them together, that you get something fresh out of the collision of these things," says McDowell, who was very keen to give the film an Eastern European blend. "There's no Victorian architecture, as we understand it, in Eastern Europe. So what we did was take Eastern European elements and put them together with the Victorian look so it has an edge, hopefully, that is neither Moscow nor London." Even so, some of the structures were based on real buildings, with the Church in the Land of the Living actually inspired by one in Kutna Horá just outside Prague, in the Czech Republic. "There's an ossuary there, an old bone church, and all the architecture around there has that

feel to it," says Lowry. "But we were very careful to stay away from any religious symbols. We didn't want to have any Christian symbols in it, so we left them all out. You know they're in a church because it's got big stained-glass windows and turrets."

Another key location in the Land of the Living is the dark, foreboding forest in which Victor heads off to practice his vows, only to find himself "married" to Corpse Bride. According to Lowry it was illustrator Simón Varela who produced a series of initial sketches that were very children's storybook in tone and which provided the impetus for the look and feel of the woods. "We thought it might be nice to do humped hills

OPPOSITE: Rigger Gary Faulkner putting finishing touches on the Land of the Living woods. ABOVE: The Everglot Mansion under construction.

with very linear straight trees and be very illustrative with that," he says. "So the forest is very much like an illustration. It was painted to look like an illustration, but at the same time we were trying not to make it look like *Nightmare*, obviously, trying not to make it look like *Sleepy Hollow*. We used a couple of very simple motifs: mounds of snow and dirt, upturned trees, and long, thin black trees, with an occasional flourish of Tim Burton-esque curls and ferns down at the base of the trees. We just tried to keep it simple, very clean, and graphic."

This description could also pertain to the entrance hall of the Everglot mansion, another of Lowry's favorite sets, which plays host to the film's first major musical number and which started off filled with pictures, antlers, and chandeliers hanging in it before the clutter was stripped back to reflect their financial status in the story, namely, broke. "It's got this big airplane-hangar kind of feel to it and is really dreary and empty and feels horrible in a way, but it's very elegant and beautiful at the same time. I think that set's gorgeous and has got a really nicely proportioned set of stairs that come down the center of it."

While the Land of the Living was based in different versions of reality, the design

OPPOSITE: Land of the Living town square concept by Luc Desmarchelier.
ABOVE: Color study of the bridge by Luc Desmarchelier.
FOLLOWING PAGES: Three concept drawings by Chris Baker of the Everglot's foyer and the final set.

of the Land of the Dead was restrained solely by the imagination, although Lowry says the production was keen to avoid the clichéd vision of the afterlife seen in countless movies, as well as the one Burton had created for *Beetlejuice.* "What we wanted was something that didn't feel like Hell, that didn't feel like Middle Earth, that didn't feel like a big cave with stalactites," he says. "We wanted it to be a little bit poetic, so we kept it very mysterious."

Inspiration came from an unlikely source: flesh rotting off of bone. "The architecture has bonelike quality," states McDowell, "but all of the flesh that remains on it has these strong layers of colors. So you have these very nice kind of popping of bright lilacs underneath purples, all reminiscent of flesh."

The illustrator who helped capture the eventual look of the Land of the Dead was Neil Ross. "He really seemed to get the feel that Tim and Mike wanted for the Land of the Dead," Lowry says. "We ended up designing a mysterious dark place with splashes of color, without any sure geography in the sense. So they could be in one place one minute and walk around a corner and be in a completely different place the next. It played well that way."

One of the underworld's highlights is the book-filled library of Elder Gutknecht to whom Victor and Victoria pay a visit to seek his advice on how to reenter the Land of the Living. Initial ideas for the set included a simple black void, filled with a huge gold sphere and old medical instruments. The design was distilled down and simplified to little more than a cage at the top of a huge tower, piled high with books, papers, and old scientific instruments, and on a number of different levels so that the spiderlike Gutknecht could crawl up around on them.

"Some of the first sketches [for it] looked absolutely beautiful on paper," Lowry recalls. "It was all these floating books

OPPOSITE: Victoria's Bedroom set; concept, plans, and final constructed set. ABOVE RIGHT: Nelson Lowry with Victor on the Land of the Dead set. BELOW RIGHT: Scale model of the Grand Hallway set.

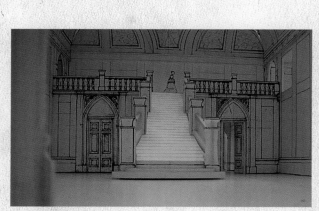

and desks and everything was in a swirl, but when we tried to represent that on film it looked like rubbish, you couldn't tell what you were looking at. You really need a sense of a real place, especially in stop-motion because the audience has to be able to look at it and think, I know what that is, I can imagine myself there, and the characters have to be standing on floors and walking through doors, it has to have references to the real world." As does another Land of the Dead location, the Ball and Socket pub in which Victor gets his first taste of life in the underworld, which took inspiration from Gaudí, old English pubs, and even a Moroccan mud look. A weird concoction but one Lowry feels "comes together nicely. It has a really unique feel to it."

Uniqueness was, in fact, Lowry's battle cry throughout *Corpse Bride*'s production. "There are so many fantasy films out there, so much beautiful work being done that it's hard to be original. But I wanted to be able to take even a little section of a frame of the film and immediately identify it as *Corpse Bride*. I wanted it to have a real signature feel that imbued every frame, and that's both Land of the Living and Land of the Dead. Pete Kozachik, the DP, made a good point early on, that they couldn't be different films, it had to be the same film, we couldn't just be totally crazy and make the Land of the Dead feel like this other planet, so we tried to tie some of the stuff together. Some of the designs of the chairs of the furniture we brought to the Land of the Dead and just skewed them a bit, so there would be a connection, as if the dead had brought them down."

While the Land of the Living is, thematically, a much grayer, more desaturated place than the Land of the Dead, the juxtaposition was carried

ABOVE: Land of the Dead building. LEFT: Concept illustration of Elder Gutknecht's study by Neil Ross. OPPOSITE: Land of the Dead color study by Luc Desmarchelier.

OPPOSITE and ABOVE: Land of the Dead concepts by Neil Ross. BELOW: Fifth-scale maquette for the Land of the Dead Pub set.

through in terms of its color palette, too. While it had originally been suggested that it be filmed in black and white, McDowell notes that, "The key is that it isn't black and white. It definitely has a range of color. It's just a very muted range and compressed to the end of the tonal scales. It's monochromatic, but you do have violets, browns, and blues. And the blacks are kind of washed out." In contrast the Land of the Dead has a lush, lurid color scheme inspired, in no small measure, by the films of Italian director Mario Bava, a big favorite of Burton's, particularly his 1963 film *Black Sabbath* and *Curse of the Living Dead* (1966). "Tim loves Mario Bava," Lowry says. "He has a lot of noir films with these incredibly strong lurid colors in them, a lot of violets and greens cutting in, so we looked at a lot of those films and were definitely inspired by them."

Once the design for each set was locked in and approved, the next stage was for Lowry to begin drafting plans for their construction. "That's my favorite part," he says. "I love being turned loose with a bunch of drawings and an art department." He

BELOW: The final Land of the Dead Pub set with Victor.

began by producing a series of detailed drawings, hiring draftspersons to translate the concepts into solid blueprints, and building a series of fifth-scale maquettes, which he says were important for the previsualization process, allowing Burton and Johnson "to get their head around what it is they're going to be shooting and how that stuff interfaces onto the stage with animator access."

And yet it was also a period of experimentation. "We went out back of the studio and grabbed ferns, bushes, branches, and plaster and just started making things without any real intent of making sets out of them," he continues, "just to get the artists' hands working and creating this organic, mysterious underworld." These models were then lit and pho-

tographed to see what worked, what didn't, and what could be exploited further, with the art department building another series of fifth-scale models which were again lit and photographed, this time with little character stand-ins. After which Lowry's art department would produce a series of full-scale mock-ups, at which stage the size of the sets began to become very apparent. "It was hard, initially, for everybody to wrap their head around the fact that these sets were going to be so big," he notes.

The reason was a simple matter of scale. The puppets were, on average, 18 to 20 inches tall, with Pastor Galswell topping two feet, far larger than those used in *Nightmare*, a result of their heads having to be a certain size to incorporate Mackinnon and Saunders' complex mechanisms, which in turn dictated how big the bodies had to be. "The puppets got a little bit bigger and exponentionally the sets get bigger," says Lowry. "It meant more stage space, more materials, more lighting."

Indeed, more of everything in fact. All told the production had around 36 sets running at any one time, with Lowry estimating they built 50 in total, although that included duplicate sets, since the production had so much to shoot and Johnson would often shoot duplicate puppets on duplicate sets. The largest of which was the Land of the Living town square which measured 40 feet by 60 feet and about 12 feet high. "I remember one day when we were working on it, I went in to take some pictures

and there were 20 people on one stop-motion set—usually there's three or four, and that's including lighting people and camera people. It was amazing. It almost looked like a live-action set, there were so many people on it." He believes the sets give the film "a live-action stop-motion look" that is unlike anything seen before, not even in *Nightmare*. "There are scenes where Victor is running through the town square at night and you imagine he must be composited into a small scale set, but he wasn't. He was running across a huge stage and the animators were either popping up through trap doors or on knee pads getting up on to the set every time they took a frame. But it gives the world a lot of volume. Traditionally stop-motion sets are very claustrophobic and small. This has big open vistas. And with some green screen and matte paintings and some wild camera moves, we've got even more space."

OPPOSITE: The set workshop at Three Mills Studio, London. ABOVE: Lighting Camera Melissa Byers, Electrician Andy Green, and Rigger Gary Faulkner working on the Entrance Hall/ Wedding Reception set.

A Digital Revolution

With stop-motion animation techniques hardly changing since the days of Willis O'Brien and Ray Harryhausen, neither has the camera equipment used to shoot it evolved much. In fact, Johnson had been planning to employ the same type of 35 mm Mitchell cameras that had been used for *King Kong* in the 1930s. But three weeks before shooting was due to start, the decision was made to abandon film entirely and shoot *Corpse Bride* digitally. Since stop-motion necessitates capturing one frame at a time, the thought had been, Why not use a still camera, specifically a digital still camera, instead.

"I was really wanting to do this for the longest time," says *Corpse Bride* director of photography Pete Kozachik. "I was always thinking I wish we could shoot without the

problems of film because animation isn't really suited for film. Film behaves funnily at night. It cools down and the next morning you come in and it gives you a different color. Or light leaks that would never be noticed in live action take their toll over time. But when I joined the show, the path was pretty much set. We were going to shoot it on film, and that was it, because all the money had been spent. Then we got ourselves a patron saint over at Warner Bros. by the name of Chris DeFaria who said, 'Why aren't you shooting this on digital? Why don't you give it a try?'"

So that's exactly what Kozachik did. He went out and bought half a dozen high-end, consumer digital SLR cameras, ran a series of tests with them, eventually set-

LEFT: The digital camera's small size and ability to shoot upside down made it possible to use as the business end of a periscope lens. Tim Allen animates as the camera tracks down the length of dining table.

OPPOSITE: Peter Sorg makes final check on an expressionistic Land of the Dead set.

tling on the Canon EOS-1 Mark II as his camera of choice, then projected the results for Burton who said, Go for it.

Production on *Corpse Bride* began June 1, 2004, and lasted through until July 1, 2005. And the benefits of shooting digitally turned out to be enormous.

"We were able to turn shots around in a few hours as opposed to waiting a day to see if a shot or test was approved," recalls producer Allison Abbate. "If the test was done by eleven, by two o'clock you were shooting another test or doing the shot. And for us that was huge, because we were very picky and we took advantage of as many tests as possible before Mike would say it's ready to go."

The technological advances also helped out the animators. "On *The Nightmare Before Christmas*, the animators only had the ability to see three frames at a time," Abbate

continues. "Now, through tiny video taps fed into separate computer screens, they have the ability to see the whole shot as they animate it. Mike could approve things on those video taps and know that the acting is right or there's no light pop. That, to me, is amazing. I don't know how they used to animate with three frames. Now they can see the whole entire shot and know how things are progressing."

The irony is not lost on Johnson. "It's interesting," he notes, "because a lot of people thought that computers and digital technology would be the death of stop-motion animation but really it's bringing it forward."

Another benefit was that the compact nature of the digital cameras compared to traditional film cameras meant that the camera rigs could get in much closer to the puppets.

"Tim loves close-ups and often times the bulky film camera couldn't get close enough to get the shot," Abbate reveals. "Here we were able to get right up to the characters' faces and hold the focus and allow the animators to act their little hearts out. Animator access is very important, too, when an animator has to get up and down a set 50 to 100 times a shot, having smaller more versatile cameras really helped."

For art director Nelson Lowry, shooting digitally meant he could check on, and, if necessary, correct the look of any frame almost immediately.

OPPOSITE: Extreme close-ups are possible because of the puppets larger scale. RIGHT: Animator Brian Hansen with Victor. The dSLR camera aboard a motion control rig and fitted out with focus drive, matte box, and video tap, appears to intimidate the puppet.

"From sitting at my desk I can get a frame from almost any unit that's out there sent through the server onto my computer," he says. "I can augment it in Photoshop, make the changes, print it out, and bring it to a dresser and say it should look like this, and that can take as short as half an hour, whereas in the past it would take days. You'd have to get film back; you'd have to see dailies. I was able to tweak stuff very quickly and very precisely and turn them back over to the dressers and get the look I wanted."

More than that, Lowry was also able to put together a quick composite to use with green screen shots, sliding in a temporary image allowing Johnson and Burton to see what a shot was going to end up looking like. "So the first time they saw a shot on the lighting station on set, they were also looking at a rough composite."

The Voice Cast

While it's the animators who give physical life to the stop-motion puppets on the production stage, one infinitesimal movement at a time, each character needs an appropriate and expressive voice to make them truly come alive. "You need both elements to really make the performance," says codirector Mike Johnson. "It really is a combination of the two that makes a great final shot."

"To make that love triangle between Victor, Victoria, and Corpse Bride believable, to make the audience really believe Victor is meant to be with Victoria, you needed some serious actors," explains producer Allison Abbate, "and we have great voices. We have

an amazingly illustrious group to tap into. They're small voices, they're very subtle, understated voices—no one is the genie from *Aladdin*."

Needless to say, Burton was able to attract a glittering array of acting talent to *Corpse Bride*, with his voice cast including an Oscar winner, several Oscar nominees, as well as a number of acclaimed comedians. Although several of the cast—Johnny Depp, Helena Bonham Carter, Albert Finney, Christopher Lee, and Michael Gough who had played Alfred the Butler in Burton's two Batman films—had worked with Burton before, there were many who were new to his world, among them Emily Watson, Richard E. Grant, Tracey Ullman, Joanna Lumley, Jane Horrocks, and Paul Whitehouse.

"I was extremely lucky to get these actors on this movie, because, the fact of the matter is, it's a fairly low-budget movie," Burton says. "I was lucky and grateful to get people to do voices for the love of the project because they're amazing actors and it excites you when you see real great actors, professional people, coming in and doing something without any hoopla."

LEFT: Black Widow voiced by Jane Horrocks and Maggot voiced by Enn Reitel.
OPPOSITE: Johnny Depp as Victor and Helena Bonham Carter as Corpse Bride.

"To have Christopher Lee do a voice, it's amazing," he continues. "And Michael Gough. When I see that character, Elder Gutknecht, and I hear Michael Gough's voice I feel very emotional. It's nice to personalize it as much as you can with these things and I've always been lucky with actors, but [here] I have such an amazing cast. You can say this about any voice in an animated film, that they do bring it to life. But when you're talking about these puppets and you see these people, they're like the animators breathing life into them. And that to me is magical."

To voice the Corpse Bride herself, Burton called upon acclaimed British actress Helena Bonham Carter, whose credits include *Fight Club* and *Howards End* as well as *Planet of the Apes, Big Fish*, and *Charlie and the Chocolate Factory*. "I was doing another animated film and Tim said if you do that one you can't do mine," laughs Bonham Carter, who is Burton's partner and mother of their son, Billy. "Originally I think he saw me as Victoria, but I thought it'd be more interesting to play Corpse Bride, because I sort of played Victoria in my youth in live-action." That other film was Nic Park's *Wallace & Gromit: The Curse of the Were-Rabbit*, but in the end Burton relented, even if he made Bonham Carter audition for the role. "It's like counterdiscrimination," she laughs. "I had to do about a two-hour audition and he was a bit coy about asking me. But I said, 'No, fine, I'll do it.' So I did and luckily, after about two weeks, he asked me to be Corpse Bride. He was very formal about it. I think it's very romantic.

"I find watching animated films that the scripts and characterizations are better than in most live-action movies," Bonham Carter continues. "This has a very beautifully written script and I always find that the better the writing then the clearer the character is. And

Corpse Bride is somebody who is frozen in
time. She's eternally young, which is a nice
paradox with being so aged in her body.
There's a genuine innocence to her and a
purity and an openness. I love doing these
things because in a way it's pure, pure acting. It's like radio. It's so nice to act something where it's not dependent on what you
look like, so you completely create a character and you're not limited by your physical appearance. It's very liberating that way."

As Victor, Burton cast Johnny
Depp, with whom he'd collaborated on
Edward Scissorhands, *Ed Wood*, and *Sleepy
Hollow*. Depp recorded his part while the pair were again working together on *Charlie and*

*OPPOSITE: The Everglots:
Joanna Lumley as Maudeline
and Albert Finney as Finis.
RIGHT: Victoria Everglot
played by Emily Watson.
BELOW: The Van Dorts: Paul
Whitehouse as William and
Tracey Ullman as Nell.*

the Chocolate Factory. "He hadn't done an
animated film before," Burton notes. "But
whether it's live-action or animation, he
always brings so much to it. What was
really strange is that the character was
designed a long time before I asked Johnny
to do it, but it reminded me of him. So I felt
quite lucky that there was a certain kind of
karmic connection between the two."

"Victor does look a little like
me," agrees Depp, "kind of a stretched-out
version. It's strange. Victor's this poor
thing, kind of a nervous wreck, extremely
uptight, extremely polite bumbler. He's an

accident waiting to happen. It's a fascinating process. Tim asked me if I'd be interested in doing it and with certain people, Tim being right at the top of the list, they say, 'Would you like…' and they can stop the sentence there, because you're in. So I would have done it without reading the script, but I read the script and loved it. It's a great piece of writing. Also I loved the fact that stop-motion was all but dying until Tim dove in there, and he's really kept it alive. It's a very specific look, it's a lot different from CG and, as a viewer, I prefer it. To be involved in it and in the process is just fascinating."

While the majority of actors recorded their parts individually due to scheduling issues, codirector Mike Johnson says they did manage to get Joanna Lumley and Albert Finney, who voice Victoria's parents Maudeline and Finis Everglot, in a room together. "It was great," he says. "You could really feel the chemistry. We've got a great cast and it's all due to Tim. I think people get really excited about it when they see the visuals, and it seems to me they're having a lot of fun with the voices."

The Animators

Stop-motion requires an extraordinarily immense amount of patience on behalf of the animators involved. "I'm just gob-smacked by their craftsmanship," says Helena Bonham Carter. "Their patience is staggering and the minutia and the sort of exclusivity of the concentration."

Before a scene can even be filmed, each animator will have to do a series of tests called a "block through" or a "pop through" of each shot. "It's a real simple test," says animation supervisor Anthony Scott, another *The Nightmare Before Christmas* veteran, "we kind of just pop the puppets into different positions to get an idea for timing." These are then shown to codirector Mike Johnson for approval before the animators move on to shooting a more detailed rehearsal that is again shown to Johnson who, if satisfied, gives the go-ahead to animate.

Animating a character such as Corpse Bride herself, required an added degree of concentration and labor on behalf of the animators because of the numerous moving ele-

OPPOSITE: Electrician A. J. Walters on Land of the Dead kitchen set.

ments involved with her puppet, including her hair, her dress, and her veil.

"Fabric is a pretty tough thing," explains Scott. "Fabrics are very difficult to control, so a lot of testing has been involved with that. You don't want to use too much wire to control it, because it fights you. Sometimes we have rigs flowing through the dress to look like it's blowing wind. Sometimes we put weights on the end of the dress just to hold it down, so the animator doesn't have to fight it too much. There's a whole series of tricks to get her to look the way that we want her to look and move."

Corpse Bride's veil, too, was equally challenging. "There are a series of wires that go through the fabric which are virtually invisible," says character maintenance supervisor Graham Maiden. "And there's wiring all the way around them. Plus her tiaras look like dried flowers, but they're actually metal. That took several months to develop. Just a simple veil with a tiara has probably taken at least nine to ten months to develop, to get it working correctly."

When several animators are working on the same character, it's Scott's responsibility as animation supervisor to make sure the character remains consistent throughout. "We did some style guides before the production started and every animator has a period where they 'run' the puppets and get up to speed with the characters," says animator Philip Dale. "That helps to get everyone sort of on the same page with the characters. And Mike has a big influence as well in that. We have the storyboards that show us the scene and what the characters are doing in that scene. But it's not just movement. It's *how* they move. You have to all be in agreement as to what the character is trying to achieve in the scene and that

OPPOSITE: Animator Charlotte Worsaae manipulates Victoria's brow. RIGHT: Animator Brian Demoskoff with Corpse Bride on her wedding march is accompanied by an overhead motion-control rig carrying rim lights to keep the veil glowing.

influences how you do your blocks and what Mike tells you. So part of it comes from the animator, part of it comes from Mike, and you try and find a common ground there."

In terms of approaching each scene, every animator will have a different method of working. "Some will act out before the shot, others will videotape themselves and try and piece together a performance that way. Some animators sort of just go for it and sort of feel it," Dale reveals. "But it's useful having the voice track, because that gives you so many cues as to how the performance should be. It's actually harder when you don't have dialogue, because then you're having to create everything. Whereas you can tell from the voice what sort of emotion there is in the scene, and so it gives you a lot to pin your animation on."

Keeping the puppets in the best possible shape for the animators is the responsibility of character maintenance supervisor Graham Maiden and his team. How long a puppet will last is dictated by a variety of factors. "It all depends on the animator and the shot," he reveals. "Some animators have very acid skin. It bleaches out of their hands and onto the puppet and can destroy the foam and discolor the fabrics. Some of the best animators in the world have got acidy skin and can't tell. They're called curry fingers."

Fortunately for those animators, the silicone skin used to cover the Corpse Bride puppets means they're longer lasting than those covered by foam latex. "The acid doesn't affect them too badly. The silicone doesn't discolor so quickly. If it was foam, they wouldn't last more than a shot."

Equally important but in a wholly different way is the question of animator access—how the animators physically interact with their puppets on the stage. "An animator has to be able to reach the puppet and reach it comfortably," explains John Minchin, set construction manager for *Corpse Bride*. "We take animator access into account from day one of designing a set. It's extremely important because if we make something and then the animator can't get at the puppet, it becomes useless. But even with all that forward planning, you will, occasionally, get a change in the script that means that the puppet is going to be somewhere we didn't expect. Then we might have to cut a trap door, or remake the floor so a piece can be taken out."

Set shift, too, is a major issue in stop-motion animation. Fluctuations in tempera-

OPPOSITE: Animator Malcolm Lamont in Elder Gutknecht's Study set.

ture overnight can cause sets to contract or to expand, producing movement that can be noticeable on film, a situation that particularly affects delicate items. "When you look at the rushes, you might see a curtain suddenly twitching where it shouldn't," says Minchin. "It's generally only a tiny amount, but you can see it, you might see a two millimeter movement on a knit curtain that is just distracting. A lot of animated films in the past didn't worry too much about things like that. They probably didn't have the budgets to worry about it."

To combat potential shift, all the sets were constructed using a solid steel frame-work, making them extremely durable. "In some ways they have to be, because of the length of time we're shooting," Minchin reflects. "These sets are under lights for at least a year. So they're very, very strong."

The Music

A large part of the success of *The Nightmare Before Christmas* was its wonderful score and delightfully catchy songs, all of which had been written and, in many cases, sung by Burton's long-time collaborator Danny Elfman, who remembers Burton first talking to him about *Corpse Bride* around 2000. Although it wasn't until 2004 that he says he received the official go ahead to compose the scores for both *Corpse Bride* and *Charlie and the Chocolate Factory*.

The process of composing the musical numbers for *The Nightmare Before Christmas* had been somewhat unusual, with Elfman writing the songs before a script had even been written, working from story conversations he'd had with Burton. "Usually there's a script first and I come in to do songs," he says. "What we did in *Nightmare* was a little bit reverse order of what normally happens. When we were starting on *Nightmare* nobody really knew what we were supposed to being doing in what order, we were almost inventing how to proceed."

However, in the case of *Corpse Bride*, the process was more much traditional, with Elfman working from John August's screenplay. Even so, he says he approached the writing in much the same way as before. "Instead of Tim telling me the story, the story was in the script and like in *Nightmare* there were some lyrics I wanted to pick up on," he notes. "John had done his own lyrics for songs, and for the first one I stayed close to the lyrics he had written; the lyrics are kind of by both of us."

For the opening number, "According to Plan," which introduces the characters of Victor and Victoria, their respective families and the story of their upcoming marriage, Burton wanted the song to have a kind of ticktock, ticktock rhythm to it. "That was a tough song because Tim wanted it to feel very repressed and rigid, and there's a certain point where if you do that too long it's not going to be much of a song," Elfman explains. "So I was trying to keep the repressed feeling of the style but still having it lift just

enough to be a song. My instincts were telling me, We have to lift for the chorus otherwise it's going to be so boring. I said, 'This is the opening piece and if the whole thing is too depressing, it really will be murder on the audience.' But I found a good balance."

More to Elfman's liking was "Remains of the Day," the jazzy musical number in the Land of the Dead pub that fills Victor in on the tragic history of Corpse Bride, a song 'sung by skeleton bandleader Bonejangles.

"'Remains of the Day' was a piece of cake because I'm into old jazz anyhow," he grins. "That's what I used to play, and so any time I'm writing in that style it's

ABOVE: Orchestra session conducted by Nick Ingman. LEFT: Tim Burton and Danny Elfman scoring the film at London's Abbey Road Studios.

real fun and easy for me. I did Cab Calloway tunes for years, and I think Tim likes the old Fleischer-esque jazz stuff as well, that kind of relates to the crazy skeleton. To me it was so clear, if you see skeletons in a band they're going to be playing somewhere between Cab Calloway, Louis Armstrong, Louis Prima, and all these guys."

Less fun for Elfman, however, was the fact he had to provide the singing voice for Bonejangles—a character inspired by Sammy Davis Jr. "I couldn't do Sammy," he states. "When I started playing around with the demo and I was writing the song I just didn't find myself falling into Sammy. It started veering off early because he was such a rough-looking character and so, vocally, he ended up somewhere between Cab Calloway and Louis Armstrong rather than Sammy, except maybe for the last note where I did my best to pull out one big Sammy ending. I found myself being pulled into a rougher, growlier voice than Sammy's and the style of the piece probably had something to do with it as it came together. It was an older feeling song than a Sammy Davis Jr. song but it's all tied together in various ways."

Not that Elfman even intended to sing the song in the first place. "It kind of ended up the same as in *Nightmare* where I did the demos and those songs ended up being Jack's voice. This was harder because Jack's voice is real easy for me; Jack's voice is my voice. Bonejangles's voice is not my voice. I wrote it to be sung by a rougher, tougher-sounding voice than mine. We actually did 23 or 24 auditions and I recorded three different versions of the song with other singers and in the end Tim came and said, Do you think you can do it? But it was hard, because whereas I could sing Jack Skellington's voice all day, Bonejangles voice was really rough. Every time I sang it, I was hoarse for the rest of the day."

In all, Elfman composed five songs plus the score for *Corpse Bride*. "The score itself was relatively easy compared to *Charlie*," he reveals, "because as with *The Nightmare Before Christmas* the tone and the trajectory of the characters was very clear and was easy to follow. Sometimes following the characters and their tone can be very, very tricky; Charlie was that way. Whereas with *Nightmare, Corpse Bride, Edward Scissorhands,* and *Beetlejuice* it's very easy to follow the tone and the trajectory of where the characters are starting and going."

"In general, when we're in the Land of the Living there should always be a sense

of it being stodgier, and so I would use a harpischord and keep it oppressive," he continues.
"Or when we're in the Land of the Dead things are going to be more jazzy and up tempo.
But when you really lay out a score of a film it's much more complicated than that.
Ultimately when you start scoring, you're following the emotions of the characters. So if it's
a tender moment between Victor and Corpse Bride or Victor and Victoria, I'm going to play
their emotions and it's irrelevant where they are. Once the emotions of the characters come
in, I'm playing the characters."

Elfman's musical partnership with
Burton dates back to 1986 when he composed his first film score for Burton's debut
feature *Pee-Wee's Big Adventure*. Since then,
he's been responsible for scoring every
Burton film, bar *Ed Wood*, and says their collaboration works so well because they both
operate in much the same way.

"Tim works completely and totally
viscerally. Some directors work totally in the
logical realm of working things out intellectu-
ally; they'll tell you what the backstory is,
what characters are thinking. I find that to be
not at all helpful, because, in the end, I also work completely viscerally. With Tim, his reac-
tions are all about emotion, it's all visceral. He'll tell me how he feels about the characters,
how he feels about a song and what it should be doing, and then I've just to go find my own
gut and dive in and find a way for it to translate over to his world.

"Sometimes it's hard to get those two places to intersect," Elfman concludes.
"Interpreting musically what's going on in Tim's mind is not a simple thing because it's a big,
weird, crazy world inside. But in the process of experimenting and finding my own instincts
I'm going to find that my instincts and his instincts cross over and merge into a single path."

PART THREE

Going Upstairs

THE ILLUSTRATED STORY

Victor, a handsome nineteen-year-old with a slightly dreamy demeanor, adds tiny finishing touches to the sketch. His Victorian-style room is filled with drawings and paintings of all sizes, mostly of butterflies. There is one prominent painting of Victor with a friendly looking dog wearing a bright red collar.

The drawing done, Victor lifts a glass bell jar. A butterfly escapes, flits around the room and out of the open window.

We follow the butterfly on its flight around the town.

ABOVE: Storyboards by Sharon Smith and David Stoten.

One man, Barkis Bittern, has newly arrived in town. He is well dressed and confident but there is a sinister scowl on his face as he saunters through town. He absently swats the butterfly away and his gaze rests on the Everglot Mansion—easily the best house in town.

A church bell chimes the first of four strokes. The Town Crier strides into the square and rings his big handbell.

"Hear ye, hear ye, ten minutes to go till the Van Dorts wedding rehearsal!"

According to Plan

PART ONE

NELL
It's a beautiful day!

WILLIAM
It's a rather nice day.

NELL
A day for a glorious wedding!

WILLIAM
A *rehearsal* my dear, to be perfectly clear.

NELL
A rehearsal for a glorious wedding!

WILLIAM
Assuming nothing happens that we don't really know.

NELL
That nothing unexpected interferes with the show.

NELL & WILLIAM
And that is why everything,
Every last little thing,
Every single tiny microscopic little thing must GO. . .

NELL
According to plan—

WILLIAM
Our son will be married

NELL
According to plan—

WILLIAM
Our family carried

NELL & WILLIAM
Elevated to the heights of society. . .

NELL
To the costume balls—

WILLIAM
in the hallowed halls . . .

NELL
Rubbing elbows with the finest.

WILLIAM
Having crumpets with Her Highness.

NELL & WILLIAM
We'll be there, we'll be seen,
Having tea with the Queen! We'll forget everything,

WILLIAM
That we've ever, ever been!

NELL
Where is Victor? We might be late!

──────── PART TWO ────────

INT. EVERGLOT DRAWING ROOM – DAY

MAUDELINE
It's a terrible day!

FINIS
Now, don't be that way. . .

MAUDELINE
It's a terrible day for a wedding.

FINIS
It's a sad, sad state of affairs we're in,

MAUDELINE
That has led to this ominous wedding.

FINIS
How could our family have come to this,

MAUDELINE & FINIS
To marry off our daughter to the nouveau riche. . .

MAUDELINE
They're so common,

FINIS
So coarse,

MAUDELINE
Oh it couldn't be worse. . . *(she sighs)*

FINIS
Couldn't be worse?—
I'm afraid I disagree.
They could be land rich, bankrupt aristocracy.
Without a penny to their name,
just like you and me. . .

MAUDELINE
Oh dear.

MAUDELINE & FINIS
And that's why everything, every last little thing,
Every single, tiny, microscopic little thing must GO. . .

MAUDELINE
According to plan—

FINIS
our daughter will wed.

MAUDELINE
According to plan,

FINIS
our family led. . .

MAUDELINE & FINIS
From the depths of deepest poverty

MAUDELINE
To the noble realm

FINIS
of our ancestry.

MAUDELINE & FINIS
And who would have guessed, in a million years?
That our daughter with a face,

FINIS
of an otter in disgrace,

MAUDELINE & FINIS
Would provide our ticket, to our rightful place?

CUT TO:

INT. VICTORIA'S BEDROOM – DAY

VICTORIA EVERGLOT. Despite what her mother thinks, she's a pretty, sweet young girl. At the moment, she is being laced into tight corsets by her elderly maid, Hildegarde.

The SONG continues, though they talk for a moment.

VICTORIA

Oh, Hildegarde, what if Victor and I don't like each other?

There is a shocked, severe LAUGH from the doorway. Victoria and Hildegarde whirl to see the imposing figure of Maudeline. Finis is at her side.

MAUDELINE

As if that has anything to do with marriage? Do you suppose your father and I "like" each other?

VICTORIA

Surely you must, a little?

FINIS & MAUDELINE *(in unison)*

Of course not!

Maudeline turns on her heel. Without looking back—

MAUDELINE

Get those corsets laced properly! I can hear you speak without gasping!

———— **PART THREE** ————

INT. EVERGLOT ENTRY HALL – DAY

Finis and Maudeline step down the grand stairway.

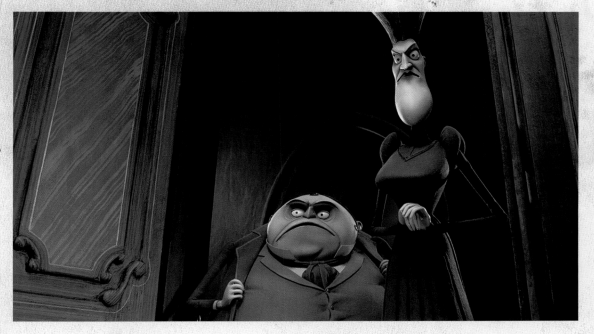

MAUDELINE

Marriage is a partnership, a little tit for tat. You'd think a lifetime watching us (beginning to sing)
Would have taught her that,
might have taught her that!

FINIS

Everything will be perfect. . .

MAUDELINE

Everything will be perfect. . .

FINIS

Everything MUST be perfect!

MAUDELINE, WILLIAM & NELL *(overlapping Finis)*

Perfect. . . Perfect. . . .

ALL IN UNISON *(to be intercut)*

That's why everything,
every last little thing,
Every single tiny microscopic little thing must go
(all in harmony)
According to plan!

THE SONG ENDS.

Victor stands in the sudden silence, unsure of what to do. Looking around nervously, his glance falls on a piano.

Victor is irresistibly drawn to it. He sits and caresses the keys. On the piano he notices a small vase holding a single stem of winter jasmine. He begins to play, at first haltingly, then losing himself in the music.

His song is sad but dreamy.

Cut to: Victoria is nervously adjusting her already perfect hair when the music suddenly floats up to her.

Victoria stops, transfixed, then continues down the steps, following the sound of the piano.

She quietly walks up behind Victor.

Victor is seated at the piano, his back toward the stairs. He plays, lost in his music.

Startled, Victor jumps in his seat, banging his knees on the piano, causing the lid to drop with a loud, reverberating thud.

OPPOSITE: Storyboards by Sharon Smith.

The group has gathered in the drawing room to rehearse the wedding ceremony. Seated are Finis and Maudeline, William and Nell.

The front of the room has been set up as a makeshift altar. An elaborately carved table holds a pair of candles and a chalice.

Pressure is high and the rehearsal hasn't been going so well.

Grimly imposing Pastor Galswells presides, holding a book and an ornamental holy scepter. Victor trembles in nervous agony as Pastor Galswells glares at him.

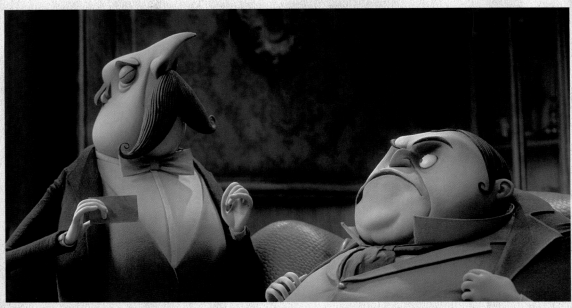

The doorbell chimes.

  Finis: "Get the door Emil."

  Pastor Galswells: "Let's just pick it up at the candle bit."

  Emil returns with a calling card in hand.

  Emil: "A Lord Barkis, sir."

  Finis and Maudeline are surprised by this unexpected arrival, but the stranger's haughty manner and dress convince them that he must indeed be of noble lineage.

  As Barkis takes his seat, he gestures halfheartedly at the bemused party.

  Barkis: "Do carry on."

  Victor holds the candle in his left hand. He takes Victoria's elbow and walks forward. Victoria takes three steps forward. Victor accidentally takes four.

  Pastor Galswells hits him with the holy scepter.

  Pastor Galswells: "Pay attention! Have you even remembered to bring the ring?"

  Victor: The ring... yes! Of course!

  He pulls the ring out of this pocket, and fumbling, drops it. Everyone gasps at this sacrilege.

OPPOSITE: Storyboards by Dean Roberts.

Amidst all the ineffectual chaos, Barkis silently extends his hand, gripping the goblet of wine. He tips it onto Maudeline's dress, and with a puff of smoke, the fire is out.

Pastor Galswells: "Enough! This wedding cannot take place until he has properly prepared!"

Pastor Galswells points wrathfully toward the door. "Young man, learn your vows!"

Humiliated, Victor stumbles out. Barkis smugly stands picking lint off his jacket.

Barkis: "Well, he's quite the catch isn't he?"

Distraught, Victor stops halfway across the old stone bridge, he takes out the winter jasmine.
Victor: "Oh Victoria, she must think I'm such a fool. This day couldn't get any worse."
Hearing a bell, he turns to the see the Town Crier parading in the town.
Wincing at the now public humiliation, Victor walks on toward the woods, chastising himself.

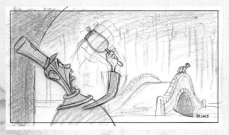

ABOVE: Storyboards by Chris Butler and Tim Watts.

"Hear ye, hear ye, rehearsal in ruins as Van Dort boy causes chaos! Fishy fiancee could be canned. Everglots all fired up as Van Dort disaster ruins rehearsal."

"With this ring, I ask you to be mine."

Spindly birches give way to dark foreboding trees. Pushing through, Victor repeats the vows desperately to himself, but his distress causes him to make mistake after mistake.

Victor: "With this hand I will take your wine, Oh no. With this hand I will cup your. . . Oh goodness no!"

He tries it again.

First one crow, then more flap from tree to tree, following him as he wanders through the darkening forest. There is a haunted feel to the forest as if someone else is watching him.

Dejected, Victor sits on a stump.

He pulls the ring out of his pocket. With it comes the jasmine—and the memory of Victoria.

Just the idea of her seems to bring a new resolve to Victor.

The cawing of the crows becomes more insistent. Victor looks up, and, realizing that he now has an audience, decides to really go for it. He stands with a theatrical flourish.

Victor: "With this hand I will lift your sorrows, Your cup will never empty, for I will be your wine. . . "

He continues his vows, this time without a single stumble. "With this candle, I will light your way in darkness..."

Victor has his confidence back. The squawking grows louder from the branches overhead. With a dramatic flourish he kneels.

Victor: "With this ring, I ask you to be mine."

He slips the ring on a small twisted root that extends from the ground.

Suddenly the crows fall silent. A faint wind rustles through the trees.

Victor looks up into the branches, where the crows silently stare down at him. The root twitches, unnoticed. Still watching the crows, Victor reaches for his ring when...

The root suddenly encircles his wrist.

114

Victor desperately pulls, ripping a mass of roots and dirt from the ground. Sprawling backward, he sees a skeletal arm clamped around his wrist.

Victor screams and flings it away as the ground splits open in front of him. A root-covered figure, wearing a tattered wedding gown, bursts from the frozen earth to reveal the Corpse Bride. The ring sparkles in the moonlight.

"I do!"

Victor scrambles backward, turns and runs frantically, stumbling through thickets and branches.

The Corpse Bride moves toward him.

Victor runs for his life, dodging between the crooked tombstones. He crashes blindly through the branches of the bare, brittle trees that seem to block his escape. He stumbles across a small creek as the Corpse Bride pursues him.

OPPOSITE: Storyboards by Tim Watts.

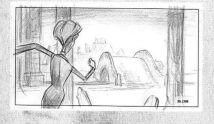

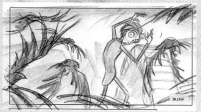

As Victor dashes blindly through the trees, the crows fly in his path. He reaches the edge of the woods and sprints toward the footbridge.

Suddenly, the crows burst from the trees, flying straight at him. He turns to run, and freezes in horror. . .

The strangely alluring figure of the Corpse Bride approaches him from the other side of the bridge.

The Corpse Bride moves toward Victor as the crows gather, swirling around them. Overcome by fear, Victor stands motionless. She slowly lifts her veil. On her skeletal hand the wedding ring glistens in the moonlight.

Huge eyes dominate her pale face.

She leans toward him, her bony hand touches his chest as the crows encircle them, forming a solid field of black. . .

Corpse Bride: "You may kiss the bride. . ."

119

"Don't crowd him.
Give him some air."

"He's still soft."

Victor bolts upright and backs up into the bar. He is reeling. He looks around the room trying to get his bearings.

"A toast then. To the newlyweds."

Paul the Head Waiter: "Bonjour! Coming through, coming through! My name is Paul, I am the head waiter. I will be creating your wedding feast."

At the mere mention of food, a lime-green maggot pops out of the Corpse Bride's eye socket.

Maggot: "Wedding feast. . . I'm salivating."

ABOVE: Storyboards by Chris Butler and Dean Roberts.

"And what a story it is. . ."

BONEJANGLES

Give me a listen— you corpses of cheer
At least those of you who still got an ear,
I'll tell you a story, make a skeleton cry
Of our own jubalishishly lovely corpse bride.

(chorus)
Die, die, we all pass away
But don't wear a frown cause it's really O.K.
You might try and hide and you might try and pray
But we all end up the remains of the day.

Yeah, Yeah, Yeah,
Yeah, Yeah, Yeah

Well our girl was a beauty known for miles around
When a mysterious stranger came into town.
He was plenty good lookin' — but down on his cash.

And our poor little baby, she fell hard & fast.
When her daddy said no, she just couldn't cope.
So our lovers came up with a plan to elope.

(chorus)
Die, die, we all pass away
But don't wear a frown cause it's really O.K.
You might try and hide and you might try and pray
But we all end up the remains of the day.

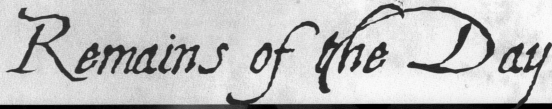

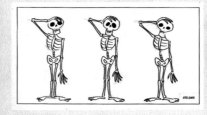

ABOVE: Storyboards by Chris Butler.

125

Yeah, Yeah, Yeah,
Yeah, Yeah, Yeah

So they conjured (up) a plan to meet late at night
They told not a soul, kept the whole thing tight.
(Now) her mother's wedding dress—fit like a glove
You don't need much—when you're really in love

Except for a few things, or so I'm told.
Like the family jewels and a satchel of gold.
(then) next to the graveyard—by the old oak tree
on a dark foggy night—at a quarter to three
she was ready to go—but where was he?

(and then?). . . She waited
(and then?). . . There, in the shadows (was it her man?)
(and then?). . . her (little) heart beat so loud.
(and then?). . . and then, baby. . . everything went black!

(Now) when she opened her eyes, she was dead as dust.
Her jewels were missing and her heart was bust.

So she made a vow, lying under that tree,
That she'd wait for her true love to come set her free.

Always waiting for someone to come take her hand
But out of the blue comes this groovy young man
Who vows forever, to be by her side.
And that's the story of our Corpse Bride!

(chorus)
Die, die, we all pass away
But don't wear a frown cause it's really O.K.
You might try and hide and you might try and pray
But we all end up the remains of the day.

 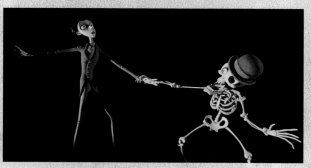

ABOVE: Storyboards by Chris Butler.

126

The Pub is swirling with activity as the Dead dance and laugh. Victor takes advantage of the pandemonium to make a hasty exit.

The Corpse Bride, distracted by the celebration in her honor, looks up just in time to see her new husband run out into the night.

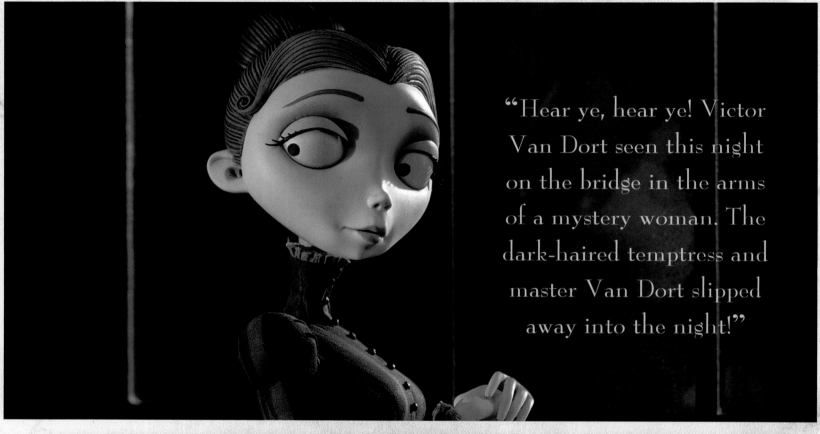

"Hear ye, hear ye! Victor Van Dort seen this night on the bridge in the arms of a mystery woman. The dark-haired temptress and master Van Dort slipped away into the night!"

The town square in the Land of the Dead is poles away from its "living" counterpart. Paradoxically, this place is filled with happy denizens going about their lively business. Amongst the hustle and bustle, the Corpse Bride searches for her missing husband.

"Oh, I almost forgot. I have something for you. It's a wedding present."

Corpse Bride and Victor approach Elder Gutknecht's eyrie. Scraps barks as they start to climb the stairs.

Corpse Bride: "Elder Gutknecht, are you there?"

As he peeks his head above his podium we see that, though bent and twisted as a tree root, Elder G. is really just an elderly affable chap in wire-rimmed glasses. If you ignore the fact that he's a walking, talking skeleton, he's not so scary after all.

Corpse Bride: "We need to go up, upstairs? To visit the Land of the Living."

Elder Gutknecht: "Land of the Living?. . . Oh my dear."

"Just remember, when you want to come back say 'hopscotch.'"

As the sparkling dust clears, he finds himself standing back in the land of the living. The Corpse Bride is at his side. She is overwhelmed by the beauty of the moonlight on the freshly fallen snow. Now that she is in love the whole world seems different.

Laughing, she dances around the clearing, disappearing behind tree trunks and reappearing again, gasping and giggling with delight.

At first, Victor is entranced by the vision of her dancing. But he is wracked with guilt. He turns away from her, reminding himself of his plan to return to his true love, Victoria.

Victor: "Hold on... Hold on... I think... I should prepare mother and father for the big news. I'll go ahead and you wait here."

Victoria sits in her armchair, frantically stitching away at her quilt, which has gotten increasingly chaotic and bizarre.

Through the window behind Victoria, we see Victor tumble over the railing. He urgently knocks on the glass.

She turns to see him on her balcony—disheveled, muddy, his jacket torn, his hair wild. She is overjoyed to see him. She rushes over and opens the French doors. Victor enters.

She truly is beautiful, with a kindness that glows inside her. Victor, whose recent ordeals have seemingly chased away his shyness, takes her hand and looks into her eyes.

They gently lean toward each other as though to kiss, but just as their lips are about to meet, Victor's gaze drifts past Victoria's shoulder. . .

"Hopscotch!"

Tears to Shed

MAGGOT

What does that wispy little brat
Have that you don't have double?

SPIDER

She can't hold a candle
To the beauty of your smile.

CORPSE BRIDE

How about a pulse?

MAGGOT

Overrated by a mile.

SPIDER

Overvalued.

MAGGOT

Overblown.

MAGGOT & SPIDER

If he only knew the you that we know.

MAGGOT

And that silly little creature
Isn't wearing his ring.

SPIDER

And she doesn't play piano
Or dance or sing.

MAGGOT & SPIDER

No, she doesn't compare,

SPIDER

But she still breathes air.

MAGGOT & SPIDER

Who cares?

MAGGOT

Unimportant,

MAGGOT & SPIDER

Overrated,

SPIDER

Overblown.

MAGGOT & SPIDER

If only he could see how special you can be.
If he only knew the you that we. . . know.

CORPSE BRIDE

If I touch a burning candle, I can feel no pain.
If you cut me with a knife, it's still the same.
And I know her heart is beating.
And I know that I am dead,

ABOVE: Storyboards by Patrick Collins.

Yet the pain here that I feel, try and tell me it's not real.
And it seems that I still have a tear to shed.

SPIDER

The sole redeeming feature
Of that silly creature is that she's alive.
Overrated.

MAGGOT

Overblown.

SPIDER

Everybody knows that's just a temporary state,
Which is cured very quickly when we meet our fate.

MAGGOT

Who cares,

SPIDER

Unimportant,

MAGGOT

Overrated,

SPIDER

Overblown.

MAGGOT & SPIDER

If only he could see how special you can be.
If he only knew the you that we. . . know.

CORPSE BRIDE

If I touch a burning candle, I can feel no pain.
In the ice or in the sun, it's all the same.
Yet I feel my heart is aching.
Though it doesn't beat, it's breaking.
And the pain here that I feel try and tell me it's not real.
And I know that I am dead.
And it seems that I still have some tears to shed.

"But I do not love him! You cannot make me do this!"

Finis: "Without your marriage to Lord Barkis, we shall be forced penniless into the street. We are destitute!"

Victoria: "But. . . Victor."

Finis: "You shall marry Lord Barkis tomorrow."

True to character, Barkis has been hiding outside the door and has overheard the whole conversation. He steps out of a darkened doorway as Finis and Maudeline pass by, and laughs eerily.

He notices the portrait of Victoria beside him. Her sad countenance looking back at him as if in judgment.

Barkis: "Oh my dear. . . don't look at me that way! You have only to suffer this union until death do us part. . . . And that will come sooner than you think."

The Corpse Bride is seated at the old piano, plinking sadly. Victor walks up to her.

Victor: "I'm sorry. I'm sorry I lied to you about wanting to see my parents. It's just this whole day hasn't gone quite, well, according to plan."

She avoids his gaze and continues playing her sad tune.

ABOVE: Storyboards by Chris Butler.

138

"New arrival! New arrival!"

"Well, she's getting married this evening."

"... I'm too late."

"Go on, get to the good part!"

Elder puts the book down on the table and opens it to a page with ominous illustrations.

Elder Gutknecht: "There is a complication. . . with your marriage."

Corpse Bride: "I don't understand."

Elder Gutknecht: "The vows are binding only until death do you part."

Corpse Bride: "What are you saying?"

Elder Gutknecht: "Death has already parted you."

Victor stands just outside the door. He can't believe what he's hearing.

Corpse Bride: "If he finds out, he'll leave. There must be something you can do!"

She looks to Elder Gutknecht who hesitates, but soon grudgingly concedes.

Elder Gutknecht: "Well there is one way."

Elder Gutknecht: "But it requires the greatest sacrifice. Victor would have to give up the life he had, forever."

Elder turns the page of the book revealing an elaborate spell. In the center of the page is an ominous illustration of a vial with a skull and crossbones on it.

Elder Gutknecht: "He would need to repeat his vows in the Land of the Living—and drink from the *Wine of Ages.*"

"My boy, if you choose this path you may never return to the world above. Do you understand?"

The Dead have gathered around the statue. Victor climbs up onto the horse and addresses the crowd.

Victor: "Gather round, gather round everybody! We've decided to do this thing properly. So grab what you can and follow us. We're moving this wedding party upstairs.

Female zombie: "Upstairs? I didn't know we had an upstairs."

Skeleton Boy: "Sounds creepy."

Skeleton Girl: "Let's go!"

The Wedding Finale

GROUP CHORUS

Wedding, a wedding , there's going to be a wedding. . .
a wedding.

BLACK WIDOW SPIDER

Hold on Victor.

GROUP CHORUS

Wedding, a wedding we're going to have a wedding. . .
a wedding.

BLACK WIDOW SPIDER

You can't get married looking like that!

SPIDER CHORUS

The spiders think you're very cute, but goodness knows
    you need a suit
But have no fears, we're quite adept, we'll have you
    looking lovely, lovely
Lovely, lovely, lovely, lovely, lovely yet.
A little stitch, a little tuck, some tender loving care.
A little thread will fix you up and we've got plenty
    as you see,
And personally guarantee our quality repairs

A little here, to fix the mess
We're going to do our very best.
When everybody sees you they will all be quite impressed.
They will all be quite impressed!

BELOW: Storyboards by Sharon Smith.

ZOMBIES

A wedding, we're going to have. . .

MRS PLUM

. . . a wedding cake is no mistake, it must be quite sublime.

DEAD KITCHEN STAFF 2

We're missing something. . .

DEAD KITCHEN STAFF 1

—Try some dust

MRS PLUM

. . . I wish I had more time. . .

DEAD KITCHEN 2

Perhaps there's something I can do, these bones might
help a bit

DEAD KITCHEN 1 *(his nose falls off)*

My nose!

DEAD KITCHEN 2

Sorry

MRS PLUM

Wait a minute. . . that's it!

DEAD KITCHEN 1

A little that

DEAD KITCHEN 2

A little this

KITCHEN CHORUS

The perfect cake is hard to miss
A wedding, a wedding,
We're going to have a wedding.

"Huzah! Hurrah! Huzah! Hurray! Our bride is getting married today."

SOLDIERS CHORUS

Huzah! Hurray! Huzah! We're going to have a wedding,
Hurray! A wedding, Hurray!
Let's all give out a cheer cause the bride is getting
    married today! Hurray!
One thing you can surely say is we will stand beside.
Until the end we will defend our one and only bride.
Our bride to be,
Our bride to be,
Our lovely Corpse Bride
Huzah! Hurrah! Huzah! Hurray!
Our bride is getting married today.

MISC CROWD

Here she comes. Oh look! It's her. . . oooh It's her!

FEMALE CHORUS

Ohhhh. . . the bride is here
She's waited for this day for many a year.

For this day, for this day, our hopes and our pride.
The bride is here, here comes the bride.
For this day, for this day, will last forever
And all of her friends, will work together
To make it the perfect day, she's always dreamed
Our hopes and our pride…
    . . . our Bride, our lovely Bride.

GROUP CHORUS

We're going to have a party like no-one has ever seen,
The Living in the land above will not know
    where they've been
The land above. . .
The party of. . .
(Maggot cries)
The Bride. . .
Here comes the bride.
On her glorious day of days,
Up to the Land of the Living to celebrate.

Barkis Bittern stands, holding up his wine glass for a toast. Normally, he'd have to wait for the room to grow silent, but it's already library-quiet.

Barkis: "Quiet down now everyone. . . Thank you. . . Elegant, Cultured, Radiant... Victoria has found a husband with all these qualities and more. Serendipity brought us together, and no force on earth could tear us apart. . ."

Suddenly the lights go out and the hall is filled with an ominous green glow. The dinner guests look uneasily around for the cause of the disruption.

The hall is in chaos as the guests stumble over themselves trying to escape, unaware that the dead gate-crashers are merely trying to befriend their long-lost relatives and friends.

Victoria exits through the front door. She stops on the front steps, looking into the village square beyond.

It has been transformed and is now full of Dead and Living holding hands and rejoicing, they are forming a procession toward the church.

The crowd noisily jams into the pews. Elder Gutknecht and Victor stand at the altar. Corpse Bride makes her entrance preceded by the skeleton girl and boy sprinkling rose petals on her path. The Corpse Bride glows with pride and happiness.

She arrives at the altar, and the ceremony commences.

Barkis: "Our young lovers together at last, surely now they can live happily ever after. But you forget. . . She's still my wife!. . . And I shall not leave here empty handed!"

The Corpse Bride looks at his face distorted with anger and finally remembers what happened to her on her own wedding night so long ago.

Elder Gutknecht: "Dearly beloved and departed, we are gathered here today to join this man and this corpse in marriage. . ."

Victoria arrives at the church and slowly ascends the steps to discover the ceremony midway through.

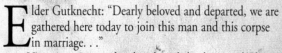

"Wait! . . .
I made
a promise."

"You kept your
promise — you
set me free. . ."

WARNER BROS. PICTURES Presents

A TIM BURTON/LAIKA ENTERTAINMENT
Production

JOHNNY DEPP
HELENA BONHAM CARTER
EMILY WATSON
ALBERT FINNEY
JOANNA LUMLEY
CHRISTOPHER LEE

RICHARD E. GRANT
TRACEY ULLMAN
PAUL WHITEHOUSE
MICHAEL GOUGH
ENN REITEL
JANE HORROCKS

Original Characters Created by
TIM BURTON and CARLOS GRANGEL

Score and Songs by
DANNY ELFMAN

Edited by
JONATHAN LUCAS
CHRIS LEBENZON, A.C.E.

Production Designed by
ALEX McDOWELL

Director of Photography
PETE KOZACHIK

Executive Producers
JEFFREY AUERBACH
JOE RANFT

Screenplay by
JOHN AUGUST and CAROLINE THOMPSON
and PAMELA PETTLER

Produced by
TIM BURTON
ALLISON ABBATE

Directed by
MIKE JOHNSON
TIM BURTON

Art Director . . . . NELSON LOWRY

Associate Producers . . . . TRACY SHAW
DEREK FREY

Production Manager . . . . HARRY LINDEN
1st Assistant Director . . . . EZRA J. SUMNER

Casting . . . . MICHELLE GUISH

CAST

Victor Van Dort . . . . JOHNNY DEPP
Corpse Bride . . . . HELENA BONHAM CARTER
Victoria Everglot . . . . EMILY WATSON
Nell Van Dort/Hildegarde . . . . TRACEY ULLMAN
William Van Dort/Mayhew/
    Paul The Head Waiter . . . . PAUL WHITEHOUSE
Maudeline Everglot . . . . JOANNA LUMLEY
Finis Everglot . . . . ALBERT FINNEY
Barkis Bittern . . . . RICHARD E. GRANT
Pastor Galswells . . . . CHRISTOPHER LEE
Elder Gutknecht . . . . MICHAEL GOUGH
Black Widow Spider/Mrs. Plum . . . . JANE HORROCKS
Maggot/Town Crier . . . . ENN REITEL
General Bonesapart . . . . DEEP ROY
Bonejangles . . . . DANNY ELFMAN
Emil . . . . STEPHEN BALLANTYNE
Solemn Village Boy . . . . LISA KAY

ANIMATION

Animation Supervisor . . . . ANTHONY SCOTT

Animators . . . . PHIL DALE
BRIAN DEMOSKOFF
DREW LIGHTFOOT
CHARLOTTE WORSAAE
PETE DODD
JO CHALKLEY
MARK WARING
ANTHONY FARQUHAR-SMITH
MALCOLM LAMONT
CHRIS STENNER
BRAD SCHIFF
TIM WATTS
JASON STALMAN
BRIAN HANSEN
MATT PALMER
CHRIS TICHBORNE
TIM ALLEN
TOBIAS FOURACRE
TREY THOMAS
JENS JONATHAN GULLIKSEN
ANTONY ELWORTHY
MIKE COTTEE
STEFANO CASSINI
CHRIS TOOTELL

Staff Assistants . . . . CAROLINE HAMANN
OLIVER SMYTH
2D Animators . . . . MICHAEL SCHLINGMANN
JORIS VAN HULZEN

STORY

Head of Story . . . . JEFFREY LYNCH
Storyboard Artists . . . . CHRIS BUTLER
PATRICK COLLINS
DEAN ROBERTS
SHARON SMITH
DAVID STOTEN
TIM WATTS
Additional Storyboard Artists . . . . ALEX HILLKURTZ
ANDREAS VON ANDRIAN
ALBERTO MIELGO
BRENDAN HOUGHTON
MIKE CACHUELA
MATT JONES
KAZ

CREDITS

Staff Assistant . . . . EMILY MANTELL
Character Designers . . . . JORDI GRANGEL
CARLES BURGES
HUY VU

ART DEPARTMENT

Art Department Supervisor . . . . RODDY MacDONALD
Set Construction Production Manager . . . . JON MINCHIN
Lead Painters . . . . FRANCESCA MAXWELL
KATY CLARKE
Painters . . . . TONY TRAVIS
LAURA TREEN
DANIELLE MULLINS
Modellers . . . . ANDY BAKER
JAMES BARR
STEVIE BETTLES
ALICE BIRD
MICK CHIPPINGTON
MARK CORDORY
CHARLES FLETCHER
MIKE GOULD
ANDREW HOWARD GREEN
MARK GUNNING
NICOLA HATCH
CHRIS HEPPLE
VALMA HIBLEN
PENNY HOWARTH
BARRY JONES
OLIVER JONES
CLARE KINROSS
AMY MABIRE
IAN MacCABE
THECLA MALLINSON
MARTIN MATTINGLEY
CATHY MAZE
STEVE McCLURE
CORMAC McKEE
ANGELA PANG
WENDY PAYNE
GAVIN RICHARDS
STEVEN RILEY
WILL SUMPTER
HILARY UTTING
SARAH WELLS
TERRY WHITEHOUSE
DAN WRIGHT

Illustrators . . . . CHRIS BAKER
NEIL ROSS
Researcher . . . . PRISCILLA ELLIOTT
Draughtsmen . . . . POPPY LUARD
HANNAH MOSELEY
Graphic Designer . . . . PAUL McBRIDE
Character Colorist . . . . ANNIE ELVIN
Visual Development Artists . . . . SIMÓN VARELA
SEAN MATHIESEN
LUC DESMARCHELIER
Staff Assistants . . . . CONOR O'GORMAN
SAM PAGE
KATY MOORE KOZACHIK

Camera Department

Lighting Cameramen . . . . MELISSA BYERS
JAMIE DANIELS
STUART GALLOWAY
MALCOLM HADLEY
SIMON JACOBS
JAMES LEWIS
SIMON PAUL
GRAHAM PETTIT
PETER SORG
MARK STEWART
Camera Assistants . . . . RUPERT DAVIES
MATT DAY
CHRISTOPHE LEIGNEL
BETH MacDONALD
MARK NUTKINS
GEOFF ROBBINS
MARK SWAFFIELD
CAROLINE WILSON
MoCo Supervisor . . . . ANDY BOWMAN
MoCo Technician . . . . ROBERTA TROUTON

Lighting

Chief Lighting Technician . . . . CLIVE SCOTT
Assistant Chief Lighting Technicians . . . . DEAN FORD
GARY WELCH
AARON WALTERS
DAVID GENGE
ROBERT COLLINS
TOM GUY
ANDY GREEN

Assistant Chief Lighting Technicians (cont.) ADAM MASLOWSKI
EDGAR ALBERTO

Puppets Made by . . . . MACKINNON AND SAUNDERS
IAN MACKINNON
PETER SAUNDERS
Project Supervisor . . . . KAT ALIOSHIN
Lead Sculptor . . . . NOEL BAKER
Lead Paint . . . . NICK ROBERSON
Lead Armature . . . . GEORGINA HAYNS
Lead Costumes . . . . MICHELLE SCATTERGOOD
Lead Foam . . . . BETHAN JONES
Lead Mould . . . . BRIDGET SMITH
Lead Fabrication . . . . CHRISTINE KEOGH
Lead Silicone . . . . MARK THOMPSON
Puppet Modelers . . . . MIKE ASQUITH
EMILY AUSTEN
COLIN BATTY
CHRIS BOOTH
FIONA BUNTING
CARRIE CLARKE
RUTH CURTIS
MARK EVANS
ANTHONY FALLOWS
ANGELA FRANKHAM
BEN GREENWOOD
GRAEME HALL
ANNE HALL
JOE HOLMAN
REBECCA HUNT
CLARE JONES
YEE-MEE LI
COLIN MACKINNON
ROBBIE MANNING
SPENCER MARSDEN
RICHARD MILES
SARA MULLOCK
MEGUMI OGO
CORDELIA O'NEILL
REBECCA REDHEAD
GARETH RICHARDS
SUSAN ROBSON
JEREMY RYDER
KEVIN SCILLITOE

Puppet Modelers (cont.) . . . . NICK SMALLEY RAMSDALE
NEIL SUTCLIFFE
STUART SUTCLIFFE
AMANDA THOMAS
EMMA TRIMBLE
JOHN TURNBULL
JUSTIN VIRDI
CHRISTINE WALKER
SIMON WHITE
DAVID WHITING

On Set Puppet Fabrication

Puppet Fabrication Supervisor . . . . GRAHAM G. MAIDEN
Puppet Coordinator . . . . LIBBY WATSON
Puppet Modelers . . . . FIONA BARTY
RICHARD BLAKEY
DEBORAH COOK
NIGEL CORNFORD
GEORGIE EVERARD
MICHELE GELORMINI
JONATHAN GRIMSHAW
MAGGIE HADEN
JANET KNECHTEL
THALIA LANE
ANDY LEE
LARA LODATO
SHANNON O'NEILL
RICHARD PICKERSGILL
CAROLINE WALLACE
ADAM WRIGHT
Painters . . . . ASTRIG AKSERALIAN
JAMIE CARRUTHERS
LUCY GRANNON
ANGELA KIELY
RICHARD JEFFERS
Junior Modelers . . . . GARY CHERRINGTON
JOSEPH NOWAKOWSKI
Puppet Wrangler . . . . DAN PASCALL
Junior Puppet Wrangler . . . . TREVOR POULSUM
Lead Model Rigger . . . . ANDY GENT
Model Riggers . . . . GARY FAULKNER
DENIS RUSSO
Armatures . . . . MERRICK CHENEY

Production

Assistant to Producer . . . . JULES COLLINGS
Assistant to Director . . . . MARK MILLER
Production Coordinators . . . . . . VICTORIA BUGS HARTLEY
FLEUR JAGO
Animation Coordinator . . . . PORTIA WILSON
2nd AD . . . . MIKE COLLEY
3rd AD . . . . JOE BARLOW
Assistant Production Coordinators . . . . . CHARLOTTE OWEN
MICHELLE FRASER
Production Coordinators US . . . . SARAH FEELEY
DALE A. SMITH
Staff Assistants . . . . LUCY BRAITHWAITE
ANDREA CARTER
SHERRY COLLINS
JOANNE EVANS
EMMA LO GATTO
MOLLY GILBERT
JOANNE HUGHES
TIM HUTTON
MELANIE JONES
NATHAN KERRY
BEN MANTLE
CHARLOTTE PATTEN
KARYNA SANDER
PAUL SPICER
SIMON TATUM

Accounts

Production Accountant . . . . JEFFREY BROOM
Assistant Production Accountants . . . . JEFFREY BRUCE
JAMES BROOM

Casting

Casting Associate . . . . GABY KESTER
US Casting Consultant . . . . RUTH LAMBERT

Editorial

1st Assistant Editors . . . . RALPH FOSTER
EMMA GAFFNEY
CLAUS WEHLISCH
2nd Assistant Editor . . . . CLAIRE DODGSON
VFX Editor . . . . WILLIAM CAMPBELL
Assistant VFX Editor . . . . ALED ROBINSON
Digital Conform Editor . . . . THOMAS URBYE

Assistant Editors . . . . CARLOS DOMEQUE
RICHARD OVERALL
Track Reader . . . . JANE HODGE

Sound

Sound Designers . . . . MARTIN CANTWELL
STEVE BOEDDEKER
Supervising Sound Editor . . . . EDDY JOSEPH, MPSE
Dialogue Editors . . . . TONY CURRIE
COLIN RITCHIE, MPSE
Foley Supervisor . . . . HARRY BARNES
Foley Editor . . . . SIMON CHASE
Assistant Sound Editor . . . . DAVE MACKIE
Foley Mixer . . . . PHILLIP BARRETT
Foley Artists . . . . PAUL HANK
IAN WAGGOT
Production Mixers . . . . SANDY BUCHANAN
PAUL LANGWADE
RUPERT COULSON
Re-recording Mixers . . . . MICHAEL SEMANICK
MIKE PRESTWOOD SMITH
CHRIS BURDON
Mix Techs . . . . VINCENT COSSON
DOUG COOPER
PHILLIP MARK FREUDENFELD
STEVE HANCOCK

Scoring

Supervising Orchestrator . . . . STEVE BARTEK
Orchestrations . . . . EDGARDO SIMONE
DAVID SLONAKER
Score Conducted by . . . . NICK INGMAN
Score Recorded and Mixed by . . . . DENNIS SANDS
Supervising Music Programmer . . . . MARC MANN
Score Programmer . . . . JAKE JACKSON
Music Editors . . . . MIKE HIGHAM
SHIE ROZOW, MPSE
Assistant Music Editor . . . . SAM SOUTHWICK

VFX

VFX Supervisor . . . . PETE KOZACHIK
VFX Consultant . . . . CHRIS WATTS
Digital Grade Supervisor . . . . BEGOÑA LOPEZ

154

Technical Support . . . . STEWART ANDERSON
MARTYN GEORGE SIDDIQUI
NICK CANNON
ROLAND WATSON
DAVID LLOYD
MARTIN WEAVER

IT

Digital Systems Supervisor . . . . MARTIN PELHAM
Digital Systems Administrator . . . . JOSHUA McABBAN
Data Wranglers . . . . RUPERT DAVIES
MARTIN PENGELLY-PHILLIPS
SARAH THOMPSON
Staff Assistant . . . . CAROLINE ROWLANDS

Post Production

Post Production Supervisor . . . . JESSIE THIELE
Post Production Coordinator . . . . KATIE REYNOLDS
Assistant Post Production Coordinator . . HOLLY THORNTON
Staff Assistant . . . . NATASHA WESTLAKE

Visual Effects by THE MOVING PICTURE COMPANY
VFX Supervisor . . . . JESSICA NORMAN
CG Supervisor . . . . PETER MUYZERS
Visual Effects Producers . . . . GIL JAMES
LOREA HOYE
Visual Effects Coordinator . . . . JAMES PROSSER
VFX Executive Producers . . . . MICHAEL ELSON
MARTIN HOBBS
Compositing Supervisors . . . . SHEILA GORMAN
DOUG LARMOUR
CG Team . . . . PHILIP BORG
ISABEL CODY
ANDRE DE SOUZA
ANDY FRASER
NICOLAS SECK
ROXANNE NEWSHAM
NEIL ROCHE
ALEXANDER SEAMAN
MOHAMED 'MO' SOBHY
PENN STEVENS
JOERN WEISSPFENNIG
Compositing Team . . . . MURRAY BARBER
JOLENE McCAFFREY

Compositing Team (cont.) . . . . KIRSTY LAMB
JUDY BARR
ANDRE BRIZARD
DELPHINE BURATTI
LORAINE "LOLLY" COOPER
VINCE GOODSELL
KIM GORDON
NIC HODGKINSON
TOM KIMBERLEY
NATALIE MacDONALD
PHIL MAN
SALIMA NEEDHAM
DYLAN OWEN
SCOTT PRITCHARD
NORBERT RUF
JIM RUSSELL
DAVID SCOTT
KIM STEVENSON
MIQUEL UBEDA
Roto/Prep Team . . . . GIUSEPPE TAGLIAVINI
SERENA LAM
QIAN HAN
KAY HODDY
SCOTT TAYLOR

Digital Film Mastering by THE MOVING PICTURE COMPANY
Colorist . . . . MAX HORTON

Score and Songs Produced by . . . . DANNY ELFMAN

Soundtrack Album on
WARNER SUNSET/WARNER BROS. RECORDS

"According To Plan"
Music by Danny Elfman
Lyrics by John August and Danny Elfman
Produced by Danny Elfman
Performed by Albert Finney, Joanna Lumley,
Tracey Ullman, and Paul Whitehouse

"Remains of the Day"
Music and Lyrics by Danny Elfman
Additional Lyrics by John August
Produced by Danny Elfman
Performed by Danny Elfman, Jane Horrocks,
Paul Baker, Alison Jiear, and Gary Martin

"Tears to Shed"
Music and Lyrics by Danny Elfman
Additional Lyrics by John August
Produced by Danny Elfman
Performed by Helena Bonham Carter,
Jane Horrocks, and Enn Reitel

"Tannhauser: Pilgrim's Chorus"
Written by Richard Wagner
Performed by Simon Preston
Courtesy of Decca Music Group Limited
Under License from Universal Music Enterprises

"The Wedding Song"
Music and Lyrics by Danny Elfman
Produced by Danny Elfman
Performed by Danny Elfman, Jane Horrocks,
Paul Baker, Alison Jiear, and Gary Martin

"Tara Theme"
Written by Max Steiner

Production Consultants . . . . POSTER PICTURES

Made at 3 Mills Studios, London, England

This motion picture © 2005 Patalex II Productions Limited
Story and Screenplay © 2005 Warner Bros. Entertainment Inc.
Original Score © 2005 Warner-Barham Music, LLC

In memory of JOE RANFT

A PATALEX II PRODUCTIONS Production Worldwide,
excluding UK

Acknowledgments

The publisher wishes to thank the following for their special contributions to this book:

At Corpse Bride: Allison Abbate, Derek Frey, Jules Collings, Fleur Jago, Melanie Jones, Martin Pelham, and Carlos Grangel;

At Moving Picture Company: Gil James and Matthew Bristowe;

At Warner Bros. Consumer Products, Global Publishing: Dave Rupert, Isabelle Giggins, Kevin Bricklin, and Martha Carreon; at Warner Bros. Home Video: Mike Saksa and Jim Wuthrich;

Writer Mark Salisbury (who would like to dedicate this book to Laura, Milo, and the amazing staff of the Neo Natal Unit, UCLH);

Designer Timothy Shaner;

And, of course, directors Tim Burton and Mike Johnson, along with their remarkable team pictured here.